COPING WITH TEENAGERS

Successful Parents Tell How They Did It

COPING WITH TEENAGERS

Successful Parents Tell How They Did It

JUDITH WOLFE

Introduction by Martin Shepard, M.D.

THE PERMANENT PRESS
Noayc Road, Sag Harbor, NY 11963

ISBN: 0-932966-30-6
Library of Congress Number: 82-084009

THE PERMANENT PRESS, RD2 Noyac Road,
Sag Harbor, New York, 11963

Manufactured in the United States of America

For Daniel
Who helped me grow up
With love

CONTENTS

INTRODUCTION
by Martin Shepard, M.D.

Several years ago my wife and I led an encounter group in a suburban community. Those participating were all adults in their thirties and forties. The group met once a week on a Wednesday evening. It began at eight P.M. and was officially scheduled to end two hours later, though we often stayed in session for another half hour or so until the dialogues simply ran out of steam.

At one point some group members suggested "theme" meetings. And so we scheduled a series of weekly discussions pertaining to problems in the area of socializing, self-confidence, sex, work, marital stress, and raising teenagers. Every one of these meetings allowed the group to disband well before eleven at night until we got to that session concerning their adolescents. That discussion lasted past one-thirty in the morning, ending only because of exhaustion. I had never anticipated how many people were having terrible problems in dealing with their kids.

My psychiatric training left me totally unprepared for this. Neurosis, sexual maladjustments, unhappy marriages, psychotic behavior—in all these spheres I was well trained and well read. Scores of books written by experts offered sound guidance in dealing with all of the above. There were also volumes written about the raising of small children; about breast feeding, toilet training, bed-wetting, and the separation anxieties that could appear when tots went off to kindergarten. But where were the useful books on dealing with teenagers? And where were the experts? One thing was certain. Experts were not being turned out by the helping professions.

Nor is this state of affairs any wonder, for the truth of the matter is that, while adolescence is certainly the most chaotic period of one's life, *parenting* an adolescent ranks a close second. And one can no more readily impose order and serenity on the turbulence of the teenage years than one can calm the waters of a raging stream.

Parents may wish advice, but advice is hard to come by for we all—therapists and laymen alike—are ill prepared to generalize or supply any easy answers. "Do psychiatrists punish their teenagers?" one of my colleagues was once asked. "No," he responded. "Having a psychiatrist as a parent is punishment enough." Having taken part, eventually, in raising six teenagers myself, I can tell you that my psychiatric background hasn't helped one bit.

One difficulty, it seems to me, is the fact that everyone's training is so limited. What have we got to guide us? Simply the roles played by our parents in raising us. And these roles—good, bad, or indifferent—may just not suit the circumstances of today. Thirty years ago there weren't many divorces occurring which meant that the problems arising from being a single parent or a step-parent were negligible, nor was there endemic exposure to drugs. The "Pill" had yet to be invented, the sexual revolution was still unborn, the breakdown of authority had not yet occurred, and the Women's Movement had yet to burst into national consciousness. All of these events have had profound effects on the current generation of teenagers.

Even beside the great changes in society, one need only reflect upon the immense differences in temperament between individuals. Just as no two parents are alike, no two teenagers are alike either. Thus the role our parents played in our upbringing of necessity must leave great gaps in enabling us to be the parents of today's adolescents. As someone commented in that group therapy session that ran until the early morning hours, "An elevator operator gets more training in running an elevator than a parent gets in coping with a teenager."

Yet, for all the difficulties involved, there are parents who manage to survive these years nicely; people who've been able to maintain or—out of stress and strain—create a relationship with their offspring that is mutually respectful and affectionate. And it is to Judith Wolfe's great credit that she has had the uncommonly good sense to tap this source in *Coping With Teenagers*. In reading these first-hand accounts of successful parents, one can attempt to get a handle on how to more effectively deal with one's adolescents.

And it's all there. From the mundane but nerve-racking problems of getting kids to help out to the special difficulties of being a single parent or a step-parent. Some tell stories where—because of intelligence, foresight, or just-plain luck—all has gone well throughout the teenage years. Others have coped successfully with the challenge of alcohol and drug abuse, scholastic failures, illnesses, and great provocations.

Coping With Teenagers is a treasury of first hand accounts, diverse experiences and challenges, patient and ingenious solutions offered by those who've succeeded as all parents wish to succeed with their offspring: raising them to an independent adulthood with love and mutual respect intact. I can think of no better "primer" to—at the very least—stimulate a parent's thinking during these very special years.

FOREWORD

I had a vested interest in compiling this book. My oldest son is now twenty-two. We managed to survive his adolescence quite smoothly. Our relationship was, and is, honest and caring, I enjoyed his company, he enjoyed mine, he did well in school and in social situations. Yet I saw many of our friends and acquaintances having terribly trying times. Some families seemed able to deal with those teenage years, some just couldn't. I always wondered what made the difference? I counted myself as a successful mother, thought I probably had the right approach, but wasn't sure what it was. I considered myself lucky for getting through it all so easily.

Now at forty-three I find myself a parent again, and all the old questions are resurfacing. Could there be any simple answers? Or is it just plain luck or a fortunate genetic make-up that makes dealing with some teenagers so relatively easy and with others so difficult? Since I now have to do it all over again, naturally I'd like to know.

I started my research by looking for the "products"—young adults and adults who were functioning, interesting, happy, human beings, and who maintained close and loving relationships with their parents. As I began to speak with selected parents, they often would say, "You should talk to so and so. *They* have wonderful children." My first surprise was that there are so many people who *do* successfully cope with teenagers and so many teenagers who are responsive to their parents' efforts. The efforts, the specific ways, these people went about it all, are the substance of this book.

I talked to people in their thirties and in their seventies, couples and single parents, mothers and fathers, fashion models and farmers. The only thing many of these people had in common was teenagers and some success in dealing with them. I also got to meet many of the children themselves, fascinating examples of their parents' handiwork.

One of the parents I interviewed said, "Babies don't come with directions." Teenagers certainly don't. But hopefully some direction can be found through reading these interviews. I learned a lot through listening. These are examples of successful parents and successful children, but most of all of successful family interaction. Here are their stories. Let them speak for themselves.

JIM

"In retrospect, it's a lot easier to have a lot of rules in the beginning and ease up on them a bit than it is to be very liberal and then try to impose them later on when the child is in adolescence."

Jim is a retired M.D., now a farmer and a writer. He is a vigorous, multi-faceted man who is unafraid of change and unafraid of admitting mistakes. His two sons, Victor and Lawrence, are handsome, sophisticated, athletic, intelligent, but showed signs of "going down the drain" after they entered adolescence.

Fortunately, Jim was able to intuit what they needed: in Lawrence's case, more structure at home, and a structured boarding school environment; in Victor's case a total separation from family life for a time. Jim was able to change old patterns and beliefs in permissiveness and impose discipline and "living expectations" on his boys. It was a struggle, but a worthwhile one; the boys have straightened out considerably, and Jim feels much happier about his relationship with them and his role as a father.

My philosophy of child-rearing has changed a great deal. I used to have a belief that man was—and children were—noble savages, noble primitives, that if you don't impose too many restrictions, and let them seek their own level, they will be naturally well-adjusted, reasonable, untruculent beings. From my own upbringing, I had always felt my mother gave me too many rules and regulations which enraged me. I felt I could more readily raise children by not being too bossy, by being rather liberal. I was the archetypal, liberal parent. In retrospect, I don't think I should have been that way. I would be stricter and more demanding. It's a lot easier to have a lot of rules in the beginning and ease up a bit than it is to be very liberal and then try to impose them later on when the child is in adolescence. That doesn't work very well at all.

I'm telling the story of two children. I would say I now have a better relationship with both of them. The best is the relationship with my second son. But even with my first one things are better than they used to be. My two sons are Victor and Lawrence. They were born a year, a month and a day apart. I was very liberal with both of them, letting them pretty much do their own thing. When they were in elementary school, they were both excellent A and B students. They never gave me any grief, personally. I won't say they were sassy kids necessarily, but they were very independent kids. Vic, the older one, could be very sassy. Larry was always a pleasanter person. Vic was very hyperactive. Larry was quite placid. Vic was always competing with someone and didn't have much of a sense of humor. Larry was an easy person to get along with. He was more of a follower. Vic was more of a person who wanted to be the boss, the leader, and test himself.

I had a relatively easy time with them both though I know a number of outsiders who often said, "Boy, your kids are annoying. Don't you ever think of telling them to stop or not to do this or to do that?" And I always would say to my friends, "Well, if they're bothering me, I tell them to stop something. I can't tell what's going to bother you. I talk to them as an adult to an adult." I felt that I wasn't always being a naysayer with my kids. I had a reasonable relationship with them and I wasn't always putting the lid on them.

Not being a naysayer prior to their adolescence made me a great naysayer later on. There's no doubt about that. I wasn't trying to inculcate manners. I thought those were things that people just got automatically. I see now that without manners and without learning some of the social niceties, which I never bothered dispensing, it put them at a disadvantage; particularly, Victor, the older one, who had a lot of rough edges. The less mannered he was, the harder it was for him to integrate himself with people in a positive way. Larry, being pleasanter and possessing a good sense of humor, was not abrasive without learning some of the niceties.

My problems began with them when they got into high school and entered the teenage years. They started hanging out with friends and getting involved in the drug culture, smoking a lot of marijuana, having their school work deteriorate—all of it led by Vic, quickly followed by Larry. Vic would hang out with older kids and start to smoke marijuana. Larry would hang out with kids and start to smoke marijuana. Vic would start to fall down in his studies. Larry would start to fall down in his studies. Vic would start to truant from school. Larry would start to truant from school. They were very close, the two of them, and had a really good friendship. But as Vic became more anti-authoritarian, more rebellious, a more obnoxious teenager, Larry would start to follow. He'd see what Victor was getting away with and say, "Well, I'll do it too."

If they didn't mind me, I saw it as forgetfulness but Vic made it clear that it was outright defiance. His "forgetfulness" was clearly provocative. That was at a point where I was attempting to put down rules, for he was also in a lot of trouble in high school that last year. He had been accepted at a college (he had skipped twice in elementary school) yet he wasn't going to graduate from high school. He wasn't passing English. He wasn't doing any of his exam work. I started to post rules. *You can't go out with your friends on week nights. You can't smoke marijuana during the middle of the week. If you're caught doing this, you're not going to be able to hold a job.* He had a lot of jobs, dishwashing jobs—local jobs to earn money, which was being spent for beer, pizza, and marijuana, and hanging out with his friends.

The situation got so bad that I had a hard time keeping my

liberal cool. One of the ways it came to a head was over a bike.
I had never spanked any of my children, but when Victor took
a bike after being expressly told not to, I began to see red. He
had ruined both his bike and his brother's bike. Neither one of
us wanted him to borrow the bikes again. I saw him lurking
around the garage and when my back was turned, off he went
with my bike. Later, I see him coming home pedaling it with a
big smirk on his face saying, "Nyeh-nyeh-nyeh." Then he
starts to run away. I gave chase, cornered him, threw myself
upon him. We had a knock-down, drag-out fight. It looked
like John Wayne and Montgomery Clift in "Red River." What
this established was that I wanted to show him that I was not
going to take such blatant breaching of discipline anymore,
that I wasn't crazy enough to throw myself into the breach. At
that point he was a pretty big, strong kid. I wasn't out to really
break his neck, and he wasn't out to break mine, luckily. We
got involved in a wrestling match. I am in pretty good shape,
but I got tired; and if he were crazy enough, he could have
severely hurt me just as I might have hurt him.

What happened afterwards was a period of calm in which
he knew I meant it if I said, "Don't do this and don't do that."
But it didn't last, and I didn't want to have to resort to physical fights in order to solve the problems. However, Vic was
getting so defiant, quickly followed by Larry, that I felt that I
couldn't really contain him in the house anymore. It was con-
tributing to a total deterioration with my second son, too. I
talked it over a lot with my wife. She was his step-mother.
She could see things more clearly than I could, and she helped
me to do something which was extraordinarily frightening and
painful, which was to kick a sixteen-year old out of the house,
to say, "If you're not going to pay any heed to what I'm saying
and you're not going to do anything that you're expected to do
and you're just going to screw up, I don't need you in the
house. Go out and live on your own." Which is basically what
he did.

I found a place, a boarding house, run by a friend of mine

who would take him. He paid his room and board from money he was earning in the summer doing his odd, menial jobs. When Larry, the younger one, saw that I was not going to brook total insubordination, total shiftlessness, total no-ambition, and total provocation, he started to behave much more reasonably at home. I don't think he was willing to risk that "being on your own-ness" that the older boy was willing to do. He was still heavily into the dope scene, and even though he was getting by he was not getting by in any way that would have made me pleased as a parent. So, shortly after I asked Vic to leave, I made arrangements within six months to get Larry into a private school which is in the South.

This was a violation of every principle I've always believed in. I've always believed passionately in public education and thought it preposterous to spend thousands of dollars to send someone to a private school. But taking stock of things, I thought I must put Larry into a different ambience where there's more structure . . . structure that I never provided earlier and now was very hard for me to impose since I had been so liberal. He needed a situation where he was with kids his age who all shared the same structure because in our environment none of the kids had parents coming down on them. All the parents were rather liberal. Or all the parents felt, "What can we do? We can't do much, there isn't much to do."

Well, we sent him off to a school where it was no nonsense. People caught you drinking beer, people caught you smoking marijuana, you forfeited your tuition and you were out. Larry towed the line and got reintegrated in academic work, thankfully. He learned some manners, learned how to dress, learned how to relate, stayed sober, and got free from psychedelics, dope and just hanging out. He got stimulated enough to get interested in school work again. So, I think that kicking my oldest son out, letting him sink or swim and sending my other son where there was some structure were two good moves to have made at the time and have helped to salvage both of their lives.

It took me a long time to come to these drastic decisions, and they came, fortunately, before it was too late. I felt that people go through periods of turbulence and it always works out. I went through a very turbulent adolescence, and it worked out for me. I've seen other people go through adolescence, and it works out for them. In my life my father was a very understanding person; he allowed me to go through all of my various changes. I worshipped him for that; I revered him for that. He was not a very intrusive person. But culture is different today, children are different today. The expectations are different today. I didn't appreciate that at the time. The seductions are greater today. The problems kids face with drugs are greater than any problems we had to go through. So, I kept thinking that it'll eventually work out. Give it time. But I saw, increasingly, that it wasn't working out; it was just getting worse and worse and worse. And I look around at some of my children's friends. Two of them have been hospitalized—in psychiatric hospitals. A couple of them are just total drop-outs—school drop-outs. It isn't a very impressive record. And I think there, but for the grace of God, my children could be.

When I kicked my oldest son out, I was very concerned. He was hanging out with a young guy who was a sociopath, whom he met in the same boarding house. Vic went in at the age of sixteen to live in the city and met this friend of his, who was into hustling gay men. My son started going around with him, going for laughs, for kicks. I thought he could have wound up dead, and I was terribly worried. But I was not ready to take him back. I couldn't even though it was taking a risk because I felt that he'd come to his senses more readily out in the streets than he would with Daddy providing. All he could become is a kind of slob who does nothing but always mooches off parents. That was the way it was heading, and that was the way it headed with a couple of my kids' friends.

What did happen, eventually, was that he came back on his own just for a visit at the end of being away for a half year, saying that he felt without a good education and the ability to earn money, life "sucked." He couldn't get any good jobs in the city, and he didn't want crummy ones. He realized he had to go to school and further his education. The school of hard knocks taught him that he better get his act together and so even without graduating from high school, he managed to convince one of the colleges that accepted him to enroll him. He went back and started studying on his own without my having to nag him. In the time that he was away, I think it cleared the air a lot. Vic and I don't have the best relationship in the world. It's rather distant. He usually calls if he needs some help for something. I don't give him terribly much because I still think it's good for him to struggle. But every now and then if he's in a pinch or needs a loan or a minor amount of assistance, I do give it to him because I know at this point he's working on his own toward something. He is studying engineering, heading in the right direction, which he was certainly not doing before.

Being on his own, having to use some of his own funds to educate himself means he doesn't have money just to waste himself with smoke and beer. Being on his own has taught him a lot. Risking kicking him out was the best risk I ever took. And as far as Larry is concerned, he is in a place where he has gotten structure and learned study habits. Any of the rebelliousness that a kid would go through with an adult, he has to do with other adults in boarding school. When he comes home on short visits, we have wonderful times. When he comes home for a summer to work and earn some money, he sometimes slips into a lot of the old patterns, but I'm handling things with him differently now. I have chores for him to do when he's home. I have certain expectations of him. He has cleaning assignments, his yard work, and farming chores. He just is expected to do it and does do it. He may belly-ache about it, try to postpone some of the things, but he actually does it, whereas before he didn't.

Earlier, when Larry earned money, he spent all of it. Both

of my kids used to work very hard in the summer time. We live in a tourist area, and they had jobs in restaurants as dish-washers. This year he saved some money because I told him that when he went back to school in the fall I was not paying for his clothes and for his $5 a week allowance he gets at school. He was going to have to save all the money for both and, by God, he did it.

When Larry's in the neighborhood, he needs friends. And so, in the summers, he tends to hang out with many of the people he knew before. When he's with them he tends to fall into some of their ways. But I know he appreciates his new friends at school even more and, at the end of the summer, after hanging out and working and smoking a little bit too much, he looked forward to getting back to school and to being in a better element. So the move with Larry has been a good thing.

I haven't described the perfect situation but things have certainly been on a good upswing. I think that Larry and I have a respectful, friendly relationship with each other, where there's a certain amount of camaraderie. He's moving in the right direction in life; there's not going to be any problem with him. He is now seventeen years old. He graduates from high school this spring. He has got plans to go on to college, and things are a helluva lot better for my having come to my senses before it was too late. And before it was too late meant doing something radical, when my oldest was sixteen and my youngest was fifteen. Had I waited any longer I would have had a terrible relationship with the two of them. I would have been bitter; they would have been bitter. I would have been hounding them; they would have been resentful.

I had felt like a failure until I made my moves. I was getting nowhere and lamenting the failure of my philosophy. I began to appreciate the fact that you cannot necessarily raise kids as you were raised. And you must take into account the indi-vidual differences between people. If my sons had been book-worms, or athletes, or very tractable, or very calm, or had been in a different social element, perhaps some of my theories would have made sense.

I took my father's acceptance, his quietness, his easy-goingness, and his appreciation of me as a perfect role model. He didn't interfere. And then I also discarded everything that my mother gave me as a model—which was structure; too much structure for me. But in disregarding all of that I became very ineffectual. Ideally I should have had my father's kindness and a benevolent structure, a loving structure rather than a nudgy, bossy, pushy structure, telling you to change your socks even before you managed to take them off. Or telling you to brush your teeth as you're heading up to the bathroom. You sort of resent listening to someone always telling you to do something that you had already planned to do. I mistook pushiness for structure. I think there's probably a way of just lovingly having expectations of what someone has to do and making them do it and being tough about it, not nasty but strict. Consistent is probably a better word for it and brooking no nonsense. I confused structure with pushiness, bossiness and domination.

The difficulties I had with my boys minding me also came from my trying to be a buddy to my kids rather than a father. I never liked discipline, and I found it very hard to be a disciplinarian. That, I think, is a big mistake. If you establish discipline at a very early age, they grow up and are used to it. Attempt it later, and it's very hard.

It's so strange because I'm directly opposite in my relationship to animals. I've had a lot of pets, not necessarily my own, but kids' pets, my wife's pets, dogs. I get on very well with them. I never had a misbehaved dog in my house because I never took any nonsense from them. If a dog was jumping up and down or being nasty or making a nuisance of himself or soiling, I would just whack him. I wouldn't draw blood, but I would really yell, scream, hit, and show him that this wasn't the way to do it. The dog would learn what it had to do and become well behaved. And the ironic part is that all the dogs loved me; I would be their best buddy. Because of my strictness with these dogs and their good response, I came to enjoy them. But with my own kids I was not strict, and they behaved a lot worse than some of the dogs. And I never got the love from my boys when I was a marshmallow. It was as if I were a kind of a sucker. I think there is a lot to be learned in the way one disciplines a dog and the way one disciplines a child. If you discipline with high expectations and you don't take any nonsense, they respect you; they look to you for certain cues. Then you can have a very affectionate relationship. If you try to put the affectionate relationship first, you're a goner.

Someday my children will see that I loved them a lot, I think. I did two things that were really difficult. I kicked Vic out, which was a very frightening thing to do and which a lot of parents can't do, and yet I kicked him out out of love for him hoping that he would have a viable future. Now when he has breaks from college, he comes home. He seems eager to get back. We don't have a close relationship, but it's amicable. I like that, and it's a vast improvement instead of the testy and nasty times of the past.

When Vic gets good marks, he can't wait to tell me. When he gets a bad mark, he doesn't want to tell me. He's ashamed of it. That's a good thing because for a long time he thought it was a goof-off if he didn't get good marks. He didn't care. Now he does care. With Larry the hard part of sending him to a boarding school was philosophical, and it was difficult because it hit my pocketbook. I resented the idea of having to pay $6000. Yet I told myself that if a kid goes to college, I'm prepared to help him for a couple of terms. And so I decided, with Larry, that I wasn't going to help him with college, but I would help him with high school. That's where I'll spend my $6000 for two years. Then he can put himself through college. We begged and borrowed the money and helped him out. It was the best investment I've ever made in my child's future.

I got a lot of help from my second wife. As a step-mother

she could see things a lot more clearly than I could. I think step-parents often see things a lot more clearly because they are not as emotionally involved. My wife is a very kind person with a very clear head, not operating out of malice but operating out of just a cool assessment of the situation. However, when she was raising her own teenagers, when mine were younger, I could see much more clearly some of the interactions she was having that were messing up her relationships than she could simply because she was very involved in them. So having understood that, as a process, I could really open my ears now to her suggestions, see the wisdom of them and feel encouraged enough to act on what knowledge told me.

One of the things I would have as advice for somebody who is having a tough time with teenage kids is to separate yourself from them, which is really what I wound up doing. If they think they are so smart and if they are such know-it-alls and no one can tell them anything, say, "OK, fish or cut bait. This is my house, I live here, I make the rules. If you can't tolerate my rules and my expectations, make it on your own."

Doing that with my son Vic helped him struggle and learn what it was all about. With my son Larry it was also putting distance between us, saying, "Listen, it's not working out here. I'm going to send you to a place where it might be better." I would say to someone who is having difficulties like that, don't wait until it's too late. Don't wait until they're supposed to be on their own or the age of twenty-one when they're certainly on their own. If things are getting too hot and too hectic, think of some solutions that would involve a different environment, a better environment, an environment in which someone can learn.

FRANCESCA

"Remember, this is your door to your house, and you're always welcome here, but don't ever bring me anything that's going to hurt me."

Francesca is the mother of eight, grandmother of twenty-four, great grandmother of five. Raised in the sheltered atmosphere of a strict Italian American family, she defied them to marry the man she loved, who she always called "Dad." Hard-pressed financially, she managed to raise eight children while working full time as a nurse in a big city hospital and maintaining a happy and loving marriage with her husband.

Francesca views her problems with her children as minor: experimentation with drugs, running with a bad crowd, school-work, household chores, money, teenage romances. Her approach to child rearing and its inevitable complications was a common sense mixture of strictness and tolerance.

We couldn't have problems. I worked nights, and Daddy worked days. One of us was always home with them. They knew, and I made them understand that I had to go to work to get them the things they needed. My in-laws wanted me to take them out of high school to send them to work and I said, "No, I want them to have an education." And they all graduated high school.

Daddy made sure they did their homework and if we ever did get a bad school report, they were deprived maybe of a weekend of going anyplace or doing anything. That's how we coped with that problem.

Naturally they had chores to do in the house. They knew things had to be perfect for me. When I left the house at one o'clock, you didn't see a thing lying around. You would never know there were eight children in that house. Cooking was already started; the wash was on the line. I would leave notes, and the children would come home, and the older girls would pick up from there. The girls had to pull the clothes in because I didn't allow clothes to be left out all night. The boys had to fill the coal stove. Only my oldest girl, Marie, she used to bribe her sisters. Like, "You do this for me, and I'll give you an extra pair of stockings." So her sisters always wound up doing Marie's chores. They never told us about it—of course I eventually found out. But that was between them, and the chores got done. They really took care of things. When I came home from work everything was usually perfect.

One incident we did have. One night there was a terrible snowstorm. They were all out sleigh-riding. My husband had made a large wooden box out in the hall upstairs. They were always told, dry off the boots, stuff them with paper and put them in that box. There was a coat rack standing there to hang anything they wore on. And when I came home from work that night, I went upstairs and all their stuff was lying around. I looked at that stuff and I opened up the back bedroom window and I threw everything out in the yard—half of it landed in the trees—all over the yard in the snow.

The next morning they got up, and they went out in the hall, and I heard them whispering. They came running in and said "Ma, my boots, my coat!" And I said, "I think I saw some things hanging in the trees in the back yard." The boys were happy because they thought now they wouldn't have to go to school. But the school was right across the street so I managed to get some other stuff on them and got them off to school. That's how they learned.

They all had to abide by the rules of the house. No smoking was allowed. They all worked part time as soon as they were old enough. They contributed to the household—not for boarding money but for their clothes and personal needs. They knew at six o'clock they had to be home for supper unless they were working. And if they were working, they had to call and tell Dad what time they would be home. They also had curfews.

The children were not allowed to scream and yell at each other. They could argue, and they did over minor things. We let them do that, but they couldn't raise their voices over a certain level. Daddy would not stand for that. If they came to me and asked me to intercede I would, but otherwise I left them alone.

I taught them to always respect older people. They were taught strict manners. I always told them, "Never let me hear that you've disrespected anyone in any way. If you don't give respect, you don't receive it." And they still remember that to this day. I truthfully can say that I never put a hand to my children; I never tore at them or banged their heads against the wall. But they never came in drunk, they never came in and said they were sexually compromised, they never came in terribly late. If there were problems at night, Daddy handled everything that came up on the spot.

Johnny was our only problem. It was the crowd he was getting into. These kids smoked a lot of pot, and everybody knew it. They were always walking around half dazed and getting into a lot of trouble. And I said, "John, I can spot it, I can smell it, and if you walk into this house on pot I'll take you to a reformatory and I'll throw you in." And I meant it. I would have. So he said, "No Ma, I won't smoke, I promise."

And of course there were all the romances between them. They learned a lot about sex in school courses, but they would still come to me and ask me things, and I could tell what they were leading up to. But I wasn't embarassed. I had a lot of good books for them to read. And of course, one learned from the other.

When Gloria eloped with Ernesto she was nineteen. His people were furious. They wanted the marriage annulled. My sister-in-law was there, and she said "Francesca, my God, what are you going to do?" and I said, "The same thing as my mother did when I married your brother." She looked at me amazed. When Gloria called I said, "Come home." And she started crying and Ernesto got on the phone, and he started crying. She came home, and we welcomed them with open arms.

So, you see, the one thing I would never interfere with was their romances. I let them go out with whoever they liked. They knew that I left everything behind to marry their father. I loved him, and we had a good marriage, and the children saw that. I showed my love openly for my husband and children. I wanted them to be as happily married as we were. You can't hold your kids back in these things; otherwise you'll lose their love.

I let them do anything I knew was to their advantage. I tried to encourage them to have a good time in life. But I did say to them, "Remember, this is your door to your house and you're always welcome here, but don't ever bring me anything that's going to hurt me."

CONSTANCE

"I think my children learned through my willingness to be honest, my desire to be a good person, a decent person . . . through my vulnerability . . . through . . . hard knocks."

Constance is now in her seventies with four grown children. She was brought up in Europe. Her father was a displaced person from Eastern Europe in the post-World War I era. Her mother was an American from the South. To her parents she was very tied, very close. She lived a sheltered life of many parties and social glitter, yet with strong values which her mother instilled. When she was young she had two loves: one, the theatre; two, nursing. Both fields she tried to enter at different times but her parents prevented her, saying these were not what nice girls do. Marriage seemed the only way out. She chose a husband when she was twenty-six, after much deliberation and many beaux, a husband whom her parents told her would not earn her a good living and to beware. She married him anyway, an American, and returned to the land of part of her roots.

Here she came face-to-face with life outside the home, new customs, new types of people; great-homesickness; lack of money; alcoholism. In short, she began to experience the unexpected: life was not as romantic as she thought. And here is where some of her learning occurred. And as she struggled and learned, so did her children.

My philosophy of child-rearing was linked in a strong way to religious beliefs. I sent them to Sunday school because I wanted them to be raised in the good old-fashioned way but it didn't work out quite as I'd expected. We'd get them all dressed in their good Sunday clothes and when we delivered the boys for Sunday school, the girls sneaked away while we were singing in the choir. Whatever money we'd given them, they walked away from the church and went and bought candy and comics instead! This went on a couple of years. The Sunday school teachers strangely enough never told me. My kids did later.

I wanted them to be trained in the religion and to learn what I thought was the Christian faith. I had enjoyed Sunday school. I liked the stories in the New Testament. I was brought up by women whom I greatly admired in the Catholic Church, in a Catholic school. Catholics were great as educators. And I wanted my children to have that wonderful experience. Those nuns were really very inspiring, very beautiful women. I think my daughters, especially the teacher, Caroline, were inspired by my tales of these wonderful women teachers. But, what I wanted my children to have from the religious point of view they didn't all get it. Martha and Caroline begged off when it came to the teenage years. They didn't want to go to Sunday school any more, when they were big girls, thirteen or fourteen. They said, "Well, Mom, it would be the Christian spirit, wouldn't it, of kindness and love not to force us." I acquiesced to that. I agreed and didn't force them. Actually I think Caroline thinks back on it as not such a bad experience. She now often goes to Church. And of course, Christian has become a minister.

My oldest boy became an acolyte when he was fourteen or fifteen. He was very graceful, was able to go through all this business of genuflection, *but* it was a kind of a little act and I said to him, "You don't really believe any of this, do you dear?" And he said, "No, I don't believe a single thing." So I told the minister immediately the way those Sunday school teachers should have told me. From that day on our boy was no longer an acolyte. That's only honest, you shouldn't have somebody as an acolyte who doesn't believe.

My oldest boy, Andrew, went to an excellent private boarding school at fifteen and it did him a lot of good. It was non-denominational. The youngest boy also went away to a boys' boarding school and there he was greatly influenced by the spirit of the school, an Episcopal school. It was hard though to send them away, especially the youngest boy. We were very close. This decision was mostly because there was really severe alcoholism in the house. I said to myself, "I would rather cut off my right hand than to let them have to see this in these very impressionable years." I preferred to be alone and let them be with healthy, non-drinking people. I do believe it bore tremendous fruit afterwards. It was a cold, difficult winter but I feel it all worked out very well eventually. Christian, the youngest boy, has told me several times, "Mom, I think you did the right thing sending me off to school. Horizons have been opened up that never would have otherwise." He was valedictorian at the 100th anniversary of his school. He went on to a highly competitive college.

My oldest boy is convinced that there cannot be a God. He's not even agnostic, but his life seems very together. There are many people who can manage without any spiritual resources. Andy, the oldest, is very fortunate in that he is not only very brilliant but when he was eighteen found a girl just exactly of the same kind that he is. They are equally well-organized, equally intelligent, equally together. They have been married eighteen years. He was nineteen and she was twenty-four. He is very successful in business. He got to be a vice-president of a huge city bank when he was twenty-seven. I don't think I contributed as much as it was just plain luck. Of course, genetically . . . I chose a husband from an intelligent family and my family also had some brains.

Both of my boys are now doing so well. Andy was always testing me because I believed in the old-fashioned way of bringing up people. I had to bring them up single-handedly because my husband Andrew did not enter into the educational side at all except when he got really mad and he spanked them and beat them. I knew no better. That's how my father had done it and father-in-law had done it. All I knew was that if children were unbelievably fresh, they had to be told off so they were. Physically told. When I had problems with Andy who was testing me always around fourteen, I'd find on of my husband's leather belts. And I'd go chasing after him but he was much quicker than I. There were chases up and down the front and back steps. He would test me by being really impertinent and fresh. Or he wouldn't do whatever chores I'd ask him to do. But the problems with him were not severe.

Neither of my sons drink nor smoke to excess. Nor do my daughters. I didn't lecture them about this. My children were allowed to smoke when they were eight to ten years old. Cigarettes all over the place. You can have as many as you want. People thought I was absolutely crazy. I was absolutely determined there was not going to be a taboo about cigarettes. I also allowed them to experiment with liquor. They saw enough of alcohol without my having to give any lectures on that.

The schools the boys went to were expensive but they got very good scholarships. They were very good students. But it was difficult about clothes. They were surrounded by so much money. They understood that some have it and some don't. That is what spurred the oldest boy on to simply get out and make it. He never had a piece of clothing paid for by us since he was sixteen. My daughter Caroline also bought all her clothing starting at the age of thirteen. He got a job in an elegant clothing store and bought his own clothes at a discount.

Christian had a hard time with women, and his difficult times were due to his not having a father image. That means a lot in a young man's life. How could it not? So, Christian found a fantastic therapist. Christian's therapist gathers people around him and imparts knowledge of a certain way of life. This is where he met Betty, his wonderful wife. This group therapy has really helped Christian. The people were searching for the same thing, answers to life, how to relate better to other people. It helped him so much.

The older son Andrew was jealous of his younger brother

because Christian was so gifted musically, and a poet, and always enticed us all with his beautiful compositions on the piano. But that has spurred Andy on to make such a success in life and to leave home when he was eighteen. Part of his leaving home was due to the sibling rivalry, partly to get out of the alcoholic situation. I loved my children equally much, or I thought I did. I tried to, but my children say I showed favoritism towards the youngest. I knew I wasn't going to have more children, and Christian was so emotionally out-going.

The older boy was always more reserved. We had really nice times together, fun times, fun evenings. I remember having a conversation with Andy when he was thirteen. He wanted to be a diplomat. I said, "You know, Andy, you must be a banker. You're smart with figures. You'll be ideal to be a banker because you like to represent, and you like languages and traveling around." And he became a banker! With Christian I did not dare to influence him. I didn't know that he would become a minister. He was terribly interested in medicine when he was eleven. We bought him this plastic man with the parts of the body. And I thought to myself maybe his interest could be transferred, and it did come about, perhaps through osmosis. I'm very happy about that. It's the most wonderful calling.

When I worried about my son Christian, I prayed. I always showed him a lot of care. Although he didn't date much, I never worried that he was a homosexual. Of course thoughts like that came, but I felt I saw no signs. He did have such good male friends, but I liked that because, especially in Europe, the men have such good male friendships, more so than here I think. My oldest brother had good friends, and they all got married in their thirties—as Christian did.

With my girls, I followed the double standard. Men could experiment and fool around, but I told the girls that my idea was, the way I was brought up, that you came to the marriage as a virgin. They don't do that nowadays, and I realize that.

That was of course twenty-five years ago. I remember Martha, I said to her, "Now you are eighteen years old, I cannot police you any more. I've told you what I think is the right thing to do, and if you want to lie around in bed with men, you will lose some of the charm that I think a woman has, by giving so freely." At that time she was dating quite a bit. I have never asked her if she went all the way. She stayed out till five once. There were no curfews. I didn't say anything. I couldn't see this thing of frightening people that they had to be home at a certain time and they rush and rush and they run into some sort of a tree. I never had curfews for my children. I did have the rules of plain decency. If you want to be a slut, you choose to be so. If you want to be a clean, honorable girl, the men will respect you. Martha did go through some very difficult years when I was really frightened. She couldn't find herself. She was in college and was lonely. She let herself go to bars all by herself where she came into the hands of a pimp. She told me when she had gonorrhea. My heart really sank. I really was frightened. I had her taken care of medically and she stopped seeing the pimp any more. She went to a psychiatrist for help. She got her M.A. in Library Science. Then she began to think that the only thing she wanted to do was to become a mother and have a family, regardless of if it was within marriage. So she went ahead and did. She has very beautiful children, twin girls, and she is a wonderful mother. To go against the social rules and conventions requires courage. I approve of what she has done. She's far more developed than many a person I know. And her girls are gems. I couldn't imagine sweeter and lovelier creatures. Due to no one's credit but her own. Martha is imaginative with her children. She has gotten them into art work and has exposed them to carpentry, gymnastics, and so on. She manages so well, she's so thrifty, she lives on almost nothing. That I admire. I know what that is.

Money was never abundant for me in my married life while my kids were growing up. For the first ten to fifteen years we lived expensively, in expensive surroundings beyond our means. That was difficult, and my children alternated between blaming me and commiserating with me. We finally wound our way out of that expensive life style and moved to a more relaxed, although equally affluent area. There, there were many more types of people, and we could frequent more wholesome people. That was good for me and the children.

Caroline seemed to be reserved as a teenager. A cloud had descended over her mind. Martha and I communicated very well, but Caroline was not interested in talking. When she was fifteen I felt her rejection strongly. That hurt. In those days I hadn't had therapy, but religion had a helpful place. My girls were exposed to a non-denominational religious organization that I and my brother had been involved in over the years. We sent the girls to spend three weeks with these people in the Midwest. They came home with the practical aspects, not so much the God-side of things. The girls were inspired, influenced; and after that we began to share. It was the time of their late teens. A time when teenagers and parents tend to communicate poorly. And Caroline began to communicate. Then she went off to college and went to France for a year. That was exciting for her. She called me from Europe and told me she was going to get married! She thought I'd slam down the telephone. But I said, "We're terribly happy for you!" I congratulated her wondering if it could be the right thing. She was terribly in love with him, and he was a nice man. We'll never know how that marriage would have turned out as he died in a tragic accident. Of course, they would have had hard times, but that's better than having hard times alone. And Caroline has made a lot out of herself. She speaks four languages, is now learning a fifth—one she says is the hardest she's studied: the language of the computer. She has a good teaching job, a handsome teenage son. Her home is so pretty and elegant, and she enjoys her independence. Her appreciation for the arts—she composes music occasionally and writes poetry—and her interest in language probably stem from the fact that both my husband and I always leaned in those same directions.

When I was in my late fifties I suddenly became the head of the household. My husband was very ill as an alcoholic. I was fifty-seven, and I became a nurse. I loved taking control of my life. I had wanted to be a nurse as a youth, but my parents had not thought it proper. This is something I really loved doing, the face-to-face encounters, the work. I had become an LPN and was even on the way to becoming an RN. But instead my health broke down. I became very ill and could no longer work. My career was short-lived, and since then I've taken the job of caring for my husband. My children have always hoped for, and worked for, their father's well-being. Even last winter Caroline went to family therapy with me and her father, thinking something good would come out of it re her father, and something good *did* come out of it: Caroline and I benefited together in our relationship; we are closer now than ever.

I'm really very terribly proud of my daughters. Caroline remembers but does forgive me that I set the boys ahead of the girls, and I am sorry about that. I did it only in so far as it never occurred to me that I had to promote my daughters' education. Nobody promoted mine. I've learned so much in the last thirty years. I feel so differently about that now. I remember though there were certain new ideas germinating in my early years of child-rearing that were different from what I had been brought up to feel. For instance, after living with my husband for ten years I came to the conclusion that men and women were not so different. They had similar desires, emotions, feelings, hopes, fears, dreams. I decided that my boys really didn't have to be educated about dolls and parenting so differently from my daughters. I had seen how they liked to play with the girls' dolls and how they loved to hold them and take care of them just like the girls. So I got them some dolls and the paraphernalia that goes with it. It was a good thing I feel. It didn't last terribly long because of course the influences outside the home put a stop to that. And my friends thought I was absolutely crazy, that I was flirting with trouble: "What do you want?" they'd say. "Do you want to have a bunch of sissies?" But I feel that this helped develop in them the parenting side. My son Andy is a fantastic father. In fact so are my two daughters. I think my forte was my confidence about, and love for, parenting. I believe that is the strongest point I have passed on to my four children. No matter how many issues to be worked out or questions of life to be answered, my children have all felt parenting to be most important. They get this from me.

In a certain way there is a bond between me and my four children because we have all in one way or another grown together. I found when I became a nurse how wonderful it was taking control of my own life. My own children experienced this, perhaps especially the girls. My four children sensed my quest to be independent, and an individual. I did emphasize manners and etiquette, but when they were teenagers I began to question the conventions. My girls perhaps intuited this more acutely and have become unique individuals. For example, Martha saw a beer ad while watching TV with her girls. She noticed the male chauvinism and decided they were going to do something about it. She and her girls wrote up a petition, went from apartment to apartment with it, telling everybody what they were doing.

It is true that the family life was almost destroyed by alcoholism and that the children have little bonding with their father, but I tried to be as honest and open as I could and really as growing as I could though I wasn't always aware I was growing. I think my children learned, here again by osmosis, through my willingness to be honest, my desire to be a good person, a decent person; they learned through my vulnerability really, through some of the hard knocks.

BRUCE

"The moment you're willing to say ninety-nine percent of any-thing that's in your heart, the bond becomes real."

Bruce grew up on the streets of Chicago, a tough guy, a "scram-bler," a hustler. His son Robby was born when he was twenty. Five years later the marriage ended in divorce. Robby was sent away to boarding school when he was eight and remained in boarding schools throughout his teenage years. Meanwhile Bruce was making it big in the music business, living a glamorous but decadent life. His relationship with his son was, by his own admission, a mess, but then Bruce himself was a mess. Then the "turn around" began . . .

I suppose this is a story of my rearing more than his. The situation was that I was growing up. I was the drug addict. I was the problem child. He was acting responsibly. To begin with, one of my great fears was that Robby would turn out gay. That's why I insisted he be sent away to boarding school. I read somewhere a book entitled *Maternal Over-protection*. The result more often than not is a gay person when there's mater-nal overprotection. But my view was distorted. I couldn't see that I had any faults. I saw it only as having to do with Robby and his mother.

I was paranoid to begin with, and I had to be right at all costs. I had to control. I had to manipulate. It had to be my way. I often became enraged and even violent. My kid was a sissy from my point of view. He was everything I wasn't. He wasn't a scrambler. He wasn't rough. He would complain to me about how the boys would pick on him. He wasn't interested in sports, and I was always interested in sports.

He was a drag. I didn't like him around me. Like the play *Tribute* where Jack Lemmon says, "I may not have been the father you've always wanted to have, but I want you to know you were never the son I wanted to have." I felt that way about my son. Never was he the kind of kid I was proud of. I hated to hear about other kids picking on him. I pushed him to do things he didn't want to do. I wanted him to be strong. I wanted him to be an individual. I bought him clothes that were made in Italy and France, and he never wanted to wear them.

He was embarrassed by my presence. I looked different from all the other boy's fathers. I lived a different life. Every time he saw me I was with a different woman. He wanted to do anything he could to make me a more conservative person. It was strange because he confessed to me that all the other youngsters admired and envied him greatly because they would see me pull up in a limousine, obviously wasted, with a couple of chicks in the car. They knew I was in the rock and roll business. All of what they dreamed about, I was. And they would say, "Your father's great." But my son didn't feel that way.

I didn't have a way of communicating with my son. I used other people. I would choose someone who was a sensitive intermediary—someone who knew how troubled I was and yet what a brilliant special person I was, someone who really liked my son. I would unofficially say, "If you want to talk to me—talk to this person. I like this person. You like this person. So we must like each other." I used this person as a buffer, as a translator. It was very cruel to those people— usually they were women—because they would get attached to him, and I would get nervous with that kind of connection, and then I would want them out. Then they would be hostile to me, and they would stop communicating with him. As a result he never felt that he was capable of a valid relationship.

He felt the only reason that person was with him was because of his father. So another resentment was developed within him.

For some crazy reason I didn't really like his mother. I saw her as narrow minded and midwestern. I saw myself growing into this sophisticated, erudite, urbane, successful, person, and she was still back there in the midwest. He was picking up a lot of her ideals and attitudes and mannerisms, and I didn't dig that. I wouldn't get into putting her down, but the way that I lived and the way that I acted was a direct contradiction to all of her values. He got that message very clearly. The only way he could retaliate was, "Oh, you want to go to that movie? I don't want to go." "You want to go to a basketball game? I don't want to go." "You want to go to the Museum of Modern Art? No, I don't want to." So I would say, "Do whatever you want to do." But the underlying statement was, *"But don't piss me off."* And he would rebel. He was smart enough to sense that he did have little bullets. And those bullets used to make me crazy.

I sometimes would force feed my kid situations. I sometimes was violent with him. I slapped him around. I suppose half way to show him who was boss and the other half was to toughen him up. I wanted him tougher. I wanted him to be self-seeking. I wanted him to choose something and go after it. And he wouldn't be that way. He was considerate, and he was sensitive. He was the kind of boy who was looking to make people feel good. He was a people pleaser. He represented things that were inside of me—that I didn't like about myself. I was a bit of a people pleaser, and I hated that.

So the things that I didn't like about my son—I in fact possessed them. But I had a certain vicious side of me that overshadowed the good side. Plus the fact that I was fucked up on drugs and alcohol a lot of the time when I was around him. I remember myself visiting his school and going into the bathroom four, five, six, times and snorting coke all day long. It was one of those schools where I was very uptight. It was like going to a funeral. The headmaster was sixty-five and talking to me about my son. He was an authority figure, and I was still like a little kid myself. The headmaster found my son very special. Robby was a writer, and they published a lot of things he wrote in the school paper. His teachers saw him as an artistic boy. But I would say "You can do better than that. What do you mean you got two Bs and three Cs? Come on. Effort doesn't mean anything. It's only results that count."

It was pitiful towards the end. My entire self image was attached to everything outside of myself. My reason for being was validated by what *you* felt about me or what kind of car I drove and my accoutrements. Or that I had a house in London and a house in New York or that I hung out with Mick Jagger. And as those things began to fall away from me I became less in my own eyes and more stoned to tolerate that condition. It was sad in a way because Robby had to talk to me as a father would talk to a son. And I hated that. I resented that.

He told me I tried to drown him once when I was stoned. We were up in Connecticut visiting some friends with a pool, and I held him under the water. All I can say about that incident was that it wasn't time for me to pass the baton to him, but he was saying, "Give me the baton." And I just hated that.

I wasn't that old, and my whole world was crumbling. Then I started to straighten out. The first year of my turn around was really the most devastating because I had to get honest. I had to tear everything off to see what I was made of. I was frightened to death of what I would see underneath. I was in intense therapy, and I was in A.A. I almost died in Palm Springs of a heroin overdose. The future was very clear. I was going to die. I made a conscious decision to live. And my son was aware of my struggle. And his love went beyond the resentments. He saw a hopeless man trying to make it.

Maybe he felt he had to be supportive. Maybe he acted almost mechanically supportive like a father would for his kid. He did not try to emulate me. He was going the other way.

He was becoming more studious. He was involved in playwriting and acting. He didn't rely very much on me. He said to himself, "My father is irresponsible, unreliable, who knows how he'll hurt me next or won't be here for me?" He had developed a way of living without me.

But when I started to fight, the reality is that he loved me through the whole thing. When he saw me try to fight for my life, he was supportive, but without making a big show. I knew that the only way I could save my own ass was to get very honest with him and when he saw that he approached me with more candor. He would go as far as I would go. It was like a lovemaking episode in a way. Like when you're with a lover and this person is willing to be vulnerable and open and adventuresome, it motivates you to go that distance too. As I was trying to reach out closer, he was reaching out for me too, saying, "I'm there. I'm there. I'm there for you."

He helped me tremendously. He wrote me letters saying, "I know what you're going through." He says now that I am a fantastic person, and that he's come to appreciate me; that he knows I have great strength. He became less reluctant to ask me things or talk about areas that were troubling him—like sex. He became almost totally open with me. And the moment that occurred, it was not two people reaching out for each other—it was two people embracing. The moment you're willing to say ninety-nine percent of anything that's in your heart the bond becomes real.

About two years ago we connected very strongly. The time we're together is generally good. There are still remnants of the past. He confessed to me there's still memories of my mistreatment that he cannot resolve in his mind even though he knows I was messed up. But he sees a father who wants to get better—who wants to get closer to him, who wants to be more real. And he's able to say "Let's pay attention to what's happening now."

He realizes that he got some short deals in the past, and they hurt a great deal. He was injured grievously by me, and I don't think he completely forgives that. But he's willing to say, "I don't forget those things, but look at the relationship we're capable of having today. Let's go for that the best that we can."

So with that expression of intent on his part, I want more with him. I want him more in my life. I want to have more honesty, more feeling, more love, between us. And it's great. Today he is a model person. People that know him—his friends—tell me he's a very special friend. He's really there for them. He's bright. He's very attractive. He has a great, strong character. People look to him for strength and hope. If they're feeling strange, they go to him because they see this strength in him. He's very well adjusted. He makes sure he looks good. He projects a good image. He's straight-forward, but he does not impose his way on me. He's a wonderful boy.

Now I admire him for the way he is. He's still not interested in sports. He's not very macho, but I don't care. There's been a big change in my attitude. He grew, and I grew. When I was drinking, when I was a drug addict, I was gone even when I was there. Now my son says, "I got my father back." As I cleaned up my act I began to see things in him that I liked—and he in me. Prior to that he saw everything that was bad about me, and I saw everything that was bad in him.

I think the key for a successful relationship with your kid is that communication must be open. And not just communication but vulnerable communication; where the parents are vulnerable, where the parents admit to fears that they have, where the parents admit to not being sure of themselves, where they are willing to listen and to share what's happening to them. Because the more my son seemed to find out how much I needed him, the more I needed his support, the more it got him out of himself. He was doing something demonstrably meaningful. "I can help my father? Shit, I never thought I could help my father do anything!"

So the honest communication is very important—to be really risk taking, to be willing to say, "Sometimes I don't feel good about myself, I'm very often afraid. I have the same fears you have. I want you to turn out perfect because I'm so far from perfect." Admit to your own imperfections. The teenager wants desperately to be respected. Don't look down. Meet your teenager eye to eye the way I finally met my son.

SYLVIA

"I wanted to present a normal home life to her and to myself because mine was so chaotic and so violent. I wanted a picture almost out of a magazine, and it hasn't worked out that way."

Sylvia's daughter Allison is still a teenager. But the "behavioral adjustments" have apparently been worked through, and the "stressful period" has been replaced by "a period of peacefulness."

Sylvia is the product of a bad home life which she is striving not to duplicate. Sylvia feared and disliked her mother and doesn't want Allison to feel the same way. Unlike her mother, she left a bad marriage. The time following was confusing, depressing and financially difficult. She lived in a "fog". She drank too much, smoked too much; her relationship with Robert, now her second husband, was stormy. She had no real career and was struggling to make ends meet. Four years ago at the beginning of Allison's adolescence, she married Robert, stopped drinking and went back to dancing. She also had a new baby, now a robust three year old.

Sylvia now has the family life she fought for. Allison adores her baby brother Brian. Sylvia is teaching ballet to adults and children. Robert is a landscaper, and their charming small house is resplendent with plants. And best of all, the problems with Allison seem to be over.

My main situation has been the absentee, real father who is irresponsible. Allison has made up for the lack of contact with him by being very intensely involved when there is contact.

Then she comes home and tells us how wonderful it is. That's been a problem for Robert almost as much as me. It can roll off me, but Robert's doing the hard work at home with a child that's not his.

I kept contact open with her father. Allison visits him once or twice a year. She makes her own travel arrangements, and she goes. She likes to keep in touch with his family. They're a very loyal family, and they make a fuss over her when she's there. Her father has remarried a woman in her early forties who has never been married. She's a very controlling woman, and now he doesn't want to send any more child support to me.

Allison is defensive of her father. She takes his side and defends him because he's poor and sick. Three years ago he found out he had M.S. (multiple sclerosis), and he called her up and told her. But I feel if he's seeing her he should still be paying something.

I think our relationship is very good, but a lot of that is due just to luck and personalities. She takes things very seriously, she's probably almost an overachiever which tends to give her a low frustration level. We went through a couple of years where she was easily frustrated, but that's leveling out.

Allison is a decent person with good instincts which were complicated by teenage behavioral adjustments: selfishness, self-centeredness, etc. which I consider healthy. One needs to go through them. I was always told I was self-centered, and that was very negative. So I'm not going to tell her that because she *needs* to be self-centered. I had no center for years and years. I was afraid of my mother, and I thought that I would end up like her. It scared me. When my mother died I was greatly relieved which is not the way I want Allison to feel about me.

I've consciously tried to be different than my mother. In the first place, I left a marriage that was going wrong where my mother did not. She stayed in it for more than thirty years, and then he left her. But I effected this big life change on my own. And I had problems I had to work out myself. I didn't know what I was doing. I was operating in a fog. I couldn't see past today. It was hard for me for a long time, and Allison learned from my struggle.

Allison is very independent now. We went through stressful periods partially related to her father and partially related to her dependence on me. But I was overprotected so I've tried to let her go. I let her choose her own clothes. She stayed out at a cast party Monday night till 12 or 12:30, then the next day came down with a sore throat. I let her stay home from school because she hadn't done her school work, and she needed a day of rest. And what the hell, she never misses school. Allison is not indolent. We're starting to let her go out on weeknights. We're policing her much less.

I didn't work out of the house till she was ten, but now I'm very busy. She knows that I'm working but will still ask, "Oh, can't you take me here on Monday?" and I'll say, "No, I'm teaching, I can't." So a lot of days of the week I don't even think of what I'm going to do vis-a-vis her because I simply don't have the time. Probably in the long run that's healthiest.

My mother was dramatic and had temper tantrums which embarassed me. I have never done that with Allison. I've never made a scene in front of other people. I can remember my mother "forbidding" me—that word. I've never said "I forbid you" because she's been pretty reasonable. She's got a straightforward nature. She's not untruthful. I've tried to work on this myself. It was hard for me for a long time not to be devious in self defense.

Her friends like me because I'm younger than some of the parents and a little hipper, but I try to be careful with them because my mother was very lonely, and I can remember her using my friends—great confidences and talks—and I really didn't like that. So that, I don't do.

Allison went through a phase of not wanting to walk along the street with me, but that's no longer so. She brings more kids here now—there's more openness. She has girlfriends overnight. She's had a couple of parties, but she's at an age where there's the question, Should you or should you not serve alcohol? and I am not inclined to. I am not going to do the alcohol thing without knowing who I've got here and what their rules are at home. She is not allowed to hang out at bars. That's one thing I would not let her do. She can have a drink in a restaurant and at weddings and parties. I don't think she drinks when she goes out. She's seen active alcoholism in her life, and I think she'll be sensible. Neither Robert or I drink anything anymore. We don't smoke pot at home. Robert quit smoking cigarettes last winter, and I quit two years ago. Allison is not allowed to smoke in the house though she does carry cigarettes. But at least she's not sitting around here smoking.

She has a curfew which she has stretched to the limits. She did sneak out of the house once with a young man, and they walked on the beach. I just happened to come downstairs and noticed she was gone. She was grounded for an entire month. There was a lot of abusive language. We had a loud verbal argument. It went a little too far and even reached the point of "I hate you. I don't want to live with you. I don't want to be like you." Highly emotional, very charged, and very hurtful. But I didn't say "Allright, try living with your father." That's a phrase that is going to have to be meant when it's said, so I've not used that one. I let her get it out though it shakes me; it jars me.

Robert has a volatile temper, and I do too if I let it loose. So I sometimes let her have it, but I don't reduce myself to her level. What really concerns me is that I don't want Robert hurt because he is doing the hard work, and I don't want her to be resentful of him. But they have a solid relationship underneath. She'll come to him for advice on how to dress. She'll talk to him about academic subjects. But it jars him to be the object of disrespect. That's hard for him and for me too because I have a big priority on loyalty, and I'm also afraid that I'm going to be discarded for her father.

I wanted to present a normal home life to her and to myself because mine was so chaotic and so violent. I wanted a picture almost out of a magazine, and it hasn't worked that way. But I still want things to be nice so it's hard for me to face problems, but I'm trying.

We have an allowance system and chores. She mows the lawn, she cleans up the kitchen after meals, and she does child care. She's a great, great help. She's unsalaried, except when she needs something. Today, for instance, I'm buying her a formal dress to wear to a college prom. She works in a clothing store on weekends and in the summer, and she babysits. She put her money into her own car and she pays for her long distance phone calls. She paid for all her school clothes. She purchases excessive amounts of clothes, but I tend to be lenient because she's earning the money. She doesn't save as much as she could have. We suggest saving, but we don't police her.

We've lifted the child care responsibilities off her after school by hiring a sitter. But she is required to take care of Brian on Sundays all day. She can take him out with her and, of course, her friends all adore him. She's been very involved with the bringing up of Brian. She doesn't resent him, but I try to make sure to give her equal time.

We had some trouble at the beginning of her sophomore year in high school. She flunked a course, and she had adjustment problems. We didn't threaten, we didn't yell and scream. We did say, "You know, the marks begin to count now." And she knows that as well as we do. It also got worked out at school; the teachers helped. We have a new guidance counselor who's very good—he's actually a very creative guy—so Allison's working in tandem with a very good principal, college oriented parents and a good counselor.

I would like her to finish four years of college because I did not. I'd like her to finish and have a degree, and I think she will. She has a good mind, and she's sensible. Like me, she does a physical activity. She's into sports. They are important to her. She's now swimming on a local college swim team even though she's still in high school. She's a jock and a brain!

I'm very involved with the P.T.O. group, and I get a lot of insight into the school that way. I maintain very, very, close communication with the school, and I always know what they're doing. I know she's around a group of kids that are not involved with drugs and that are good academically. Her teachers all like her. She was elected president of her class, she's taking college level math courses, Latin and French. If anything, I hope she doesn't drive herself to too much perfection; that she has tolerance for failure or averageness. I don't care if she's not a nuclear physicist. She's thought of psychotherapy and medicine. She's thought of law because she has an uncle who graduated from law school. I have no idea what she'll do, but she'll have more focus than I did in the practical sense. And she's interested in success.

I may be a fool, but I'm not worried about Allison and sexuality. We don't talk about sex much, but I presume she knows most everything. She had a year's health class in school, and I think they went into most everything. I think she's very selective and pristine and so are her friends. She does talk to me about boys. She's had three or four serious attachments where there's a lot of feeling on her part. They've been older boys, two or three years older, which was my pattern too. She also has adult friends that she relates to well, a number of women friends of mine that she visits. She seeks them out when she has problems. And she will talk to me about her friend's problems. She tells me about her friend Mike, for instance, that his parents are really horrible, that he can't go out, that he can't use the phone, that he had to quit his job. She doesn't ask me a great deal of personal questions, but if she did I would be open. I'm not afraid to talk to her about anything.

We're in a very good period now. It feels allright. I may be deluding myself, but I don't think so. Things are going well, her self esteem is pretty good, through her school work and her other achievements. She's pretty responsible. She's a good kid and a pleasure to be with.

When she was elected president of her class she said to me "I don't know. Everything's great, but I'm almost in tears." And I said, "Well, you're overloaded. A lot's going on. It's perfectly allright to feel that way."

She sometimes still feels that I arrange too much, so I'm trying to be looser. She has a structure too. I have to allow for hers, and I expect her to allow for mine.

NORA and JACK

"You have to invent your own life."

Nora and Jack live in a beautiful old house in a beautiful old village. The house is decorated with antiques and their daughter Rima's art work. Nora and Jack are themselves artists. They are intelligent, humorous, colorful, sometimes outrageous, but as they happily admit, they can afford to be. Their three lovely daughters grew up facing the provincial atmosphere of a small town with distinctly unprovincial parents and distinctly unprovincial problems.

NORA: Mostly their problems solved themselves. But there were terrible problems.

JACK: What problems? None of them were drug addicts. None of them were in trouble with the law. They all had abortions all the time. They were doing about three a year. But that was no problem. They never had the clap that I know of. Nobody ever had cancer.

NORA: But they did have a hard time fitting into their generation and their surroundings. That was a problem for them— and they brought it back to us. There were school problems. The schools were not doing what we thought they should. I remember Rima came home one time with five Fs. That was a real problem.

JACK: You know what we did? We moved to England. When that girl came in here weeping with five Fs on her God damn report card and not even a single note from the teachers saying

"Please see me" or anything, we moved. We moved the whole family immediately. We left for a year and a half, and it was the best thing in the world we could have done. I'm very happy I had the money to do it.

We put them into humane English schools. It was a marvelous place, a beautiful place. We lived in a beautiful house. My God, there's Rima there. That's her painting over the fireplace and on that wall, and there's her sculpture in front of you. Nothing too much was wrong with her. We did have an unhappy child, but it wasn't Rima and it wasn't Kathleen. We had a hard time making Claire happy. The squeaky wheel gets the grease, and Claire was definitely the squeaky wheel.

NORA: Yes, that was a bunch of things. She's the first one, and that's very important. We hadn't thought about what kids meant, and boy were we nervous.

JACK: It was ad lib all the time. The only general dictum I had was: You have to invent your own life. This was thrown at them from the earliest days. And they have. That pleases me. If there was a theme to their raising it was that.

NORA: When Claire graduated from high school we sent her to Europe. We thought it was the best present you could give your daughter for graduation. She got over there, and she had no one there. She hated it, and us. She thought we were pushing her out in the world too fast.

On the other hand, Kathleen, when she was only fourteen decided she couldn't stand this town anymore. And it got to be so horrible I knew if she stayed in this town she was going to fuck herself up. And she came and said, "I want to go live with Claire." Claire, at this point, was in New York City designing clothes. Kathleen said, "I want to go to the high school of art and design." She did the whole thing herself, arranging to go to New York. And we let her go.

JACK: Every night I was sleeping with one ear open for the phone. Those were years of sheer terror because it was a dangerous thing to do. It was also, as it turned out, a very wise thing to have done. Kathleen had a lot of energy that could have gone bad here in this village. New York, as we all know, soaks that up.

NORA: We are kind of sink or swim type of people. Everybody gets after us for this, but we really are. Throw them in and let them swim. You've done things, you've given them things up to a certain point. They ought to be able to take it from there. If they can't, then you take them back again and do whatever you have to do—or they go on and do what they have to do.

JACK: The biggest mistake we made with Claire is that we were not strict enough. We let her tyrannize us. She expected unrealistic things of us. We were too important to her. Claire and Nora once had an actual fist fight in the kitchen.

NORA: But it didn't hurt anybody. And we talked about it the next day. I didn't worry about it at all. It was just a mother and child, and the child was hitting out at life. I wouldn't have let her hurt me. She was just getting it out of her system. This, to me, is just the way a family operates. Besides, it cleared the air. I wish I knew what she would say about it.

The kids thought they should be artists. We never told them to be artists. They simply got the idea that that was the best thing to be . . . that businessmen are shits. Jack's never held a job in his life. Rima thought she had to be an artist, and it was harder than she thought. But of course, she ended up an artist, and she's with a fellow who's an artist. Maybe Kathleen was attracted to Will because he was refreshing to her. Will has his own business. Kathleen was the last child, and she was finally turned off by all this art and literature.

JACK: Yes, Kathleen has her priorities pretty well taken care of. She's going to be a mother and a grandmother, and Will is a damn good man. I like him more and more.

NORA: They come here often, and they have a pretty good time. We have long chats.

I remember I kept a diary in 1968. Our generation had to

break the mold of hanging on to those old hypocritical ideas and statements and lives and break into a new life. This was easier for us because we were artists and therefore sort of outsiders. Artists have always been outside of their time. We still believed in the law, but we all did drugs.

JACK: We joined them there.

NORA: But we didn't flaunt it. We didn't spit in policemen's faces.

JACK: I never, never, never, trusted society, and I told them that. I believe in what you can create yourself. That's more important than all the abstractions of fame and success and riches. That idea was gotten home pretty thoroughly.

And of course it is impossible to have a better mother than Nora. I watched her throughout all the miserable times with them. Our lives were distinctly unstructured except for Nora. She is so singleminded and loving.

NORA: Claire did have problems deciding what she was going to do with her life. She went to a psychiatrist. She read a lot. She had life readings. I think we did try to push her out too fast, but as a result she's tough as can be. Everyone loves her. She has her own house, her friends; she's a great cook. She's always helping people. Maybe she should be a psychotherapist. She's still waiting to commit herself to a career, but kids wait a long time to commit themselves these days.

JACK: As long as they're happy with their lives that's what counts. It's when they're not that the pain comes for the parents.

ED and ELLEN

"We let them know all about our financial difficulties. They saw how we handled it, and they were able to deal with it."

Ed and Ellen are sophisticated people who maintain high standards for themselves and their children. When Ed's Wall Street firm failed, Ed and Ellen went through two and a half years of financial uncertainty. They faced the task of making their two teenage sons understand the gravity of the situation without feeling inferior to their peers. Ed and Ellen also demand—and get—top performance from Jon and Tim while managing to sustain a close and loving family relationship.

ED: In our case we had been very comfortable economically and then suffered severe financial setbacks. But we put the children's ongoing needs ahead of our own. The kids stayed in private school and continued to spend summers in camp. Their lives were far less disrupted than ours to the degree that they suffered less in the way of deprivation than we did during this period.

However there were things they couldn't do that they had been used to doing before. They were associating with extremely wealthy children who were able to go skiing, had their own cars, travelled to Europe, played tennis. They were no longer able to compete with the type of children who were their friends and classmates. Of course they felt insecure, but we tried to leave their life style unchanged as much as possible. We did tell them that we never wanted to hear bickering and complaints about money or how we couldn't provide for them.

ELLEN: We would all try to do things together. We took lots of walks, since we couldn't afford cabs. Our older boy Tim contributed by making cookies and cakes and selling them to friends for their parties. His younger brother Jon walked dogs. We'd save coupons and walk blocks out of our way to redeem them.

ED: And these were children who were cast among the top economic group of New York City, which is probably the top economic group in the world; yet, they didn't feel inferior to their friends largely due to their mother. She told them that everyone takes a crap, and that money is not the only important thing. Ellen and I also shared common goals, interests, loves, and we brought these into the house.

ELLEN: We tried to respect what they were—we never tried to make them what they weren't. We listened to their words. Very important—you must *listen*—not half-heartedly overhear what they're saying. We respected everything they did, but we watched them very carefully. We were there at all times for them.

ED: We have made an inordinate amount of time for our children. I think Ellen puts the children before me, which maybe isn't such a great idea, but I also put the children before most priorities. We've gone without for them, and we let them know we've gone without for them.

Because of this the kids were not spoiled. They were exposed to the best of everything, but they knew they could not have everything. They had to do chores and contribute to the household, but that was the least of it. We were demanding about their performance in school—god-damned demanding—and they did well because of this. They did well because it was expected of them. They knew we were sending them to private schools at a deprivation to ourselves.

When things turned around, they were all the more grateful, all the more respectful and better adjusted. It's made them appreciate the fact that they now have some money and it's made them respect us for pulling us and them out of it. Now, when I want them to do something, a small monetary threat goes a long way. I told Jon that if he got three A's I'd send him to Europe—so he got four A's!

Tim, who's in college now and surrounded by all kinds of drugs, won't touch any of them. When I asked him why, he said he feels too insecure to run the risk of the trouble he could get into. And I feel they wouldn't run the risk of hurting us because we've done too much for them, and we tell them so. We let them know all about our financial difficulties. They saw how we handled it, and they were able to deal with it.

EILEEN

"I considered her to be my best girlfriend as well as my daughter."

Eileen was married for twenty-seven years to a man twenty-three years older than herself, a man who she says she despised but who was attractive and "fabulously wealthy." Her two children were indulged materially, brought up permissively, basically without rules or restrictions. But they were not the neglected "rich kid" stereotypes. Eileen shared every aspect of her life with them, welcomed their friends, shared their interests, and most importantly communicated with them openly and frankly, sharing her own feelings on sexuality and love. Also, atypically for Eileen's social set, she never cared what other people thought.

Today, vigorous, athletic and outspoken she continues to value her children as companions. Her daughter Laura is married and a very successful businesswoman. Son Danny is a scientist, a musician and a new father.

I stayed with my husband because I felt the children deserved to know their natural father. I'm glad I waited. I waited until Laura was married and Danny was a freshman in college. I thought, he's on his own now. Once they leave for college that's the end of parenting. I went up to Danny—saw him in Boston—and said, "Would it really fracture your life if I divorced your father?" And he put his arms around me and he was supportive, and he said, "No, but just don't ask me, to take sides." And I said, "I never would do that." So I was divorced and single for four years before I met my present husband. Sometimes I'd have nightmares that I'd have to go back and live with that man. He was a miser, a true miser. A man with so much money and the inability to spend it. It's an illness and it intensifies with age. But there was plenty of money for the kids, plenty of money for their schooling. So even though it was not so much fun for me, the kids were o.k.

My husband was warm enough toward Laura but had a personality conflict with Danny because Danny was a strange young man—he's lovely, but he's very quiet and he's not athletic. His father would have liked a "He-Man" who played tennis. But Danny was not interested in sports. He had a good group of friends at school, was into a lot of things. He played in a band. He was on the Student Council and enjoyed a lot of brainy stuff. But he was not chasing the girls all the time, and my husband thinks of girls as a sex object. You should be chasing the girls, and in fact trying to get them in trouble if you possibly can. This is your role as a man. So I had to defend Danny and explain that he was just shy and sensitive, and that adolescence is a time when you're pulled in all directions. Since his father never had much time for him, I would dream up excursions and things to do. The kids were my life. We spent every summer at the seashore—they never went to summer camp. We had the beach house, and that was our summer. As soon as school was out, the three of us would go out to the beach, and my husband would only come out for weekends and the month of August. I always said that when the first of August came, my vacation was over because once he arrived that was the end of our fun. I loved being alone with the kids. We'd go to the beach, we'd go to the movies at night. We'd play games. We'd play canasta by the hour with the neighborhood kids, except Danny wouldn't play because he doesn't like to lose. He has a rotten disposition—he can't take losing.

Danny was very busy with student activities and good things. I usually knew where I could locate him. He never got into trouble. He played in a band—a rock and roll band—and they used to practice at our house. I loved it. Whatever I was cooking, I'd call in the troops. I loved his friends. The best time I ever had was Danny's sixteenth birthday. I made a surprise party for him. I had his friends in cahoots with me. They knew about it, but he did not. His birthday was on Saturday night. His friends said, "Let's go to your house tonight, Danny." And they drove up, and he said, "Oh, my mother must be having company."—which we usually did on Saturday night. Then he walked in, and all his friends were there and the whole band and my family too. It was a fun party. When he went to college, he came home for Christmas vacation, and he brought home a rajah's son, and he was charming. I was so thrilled to have an Indian prince sitting at my kitchen table eating hamburgers. I had my friends, and he had his friends, and we were all curious about each other. The generation gap was not a problem for me, but it was for my husband.

We always had liquor in the house, and I encouraged the kids to have a drink or two. We never fooled around with marijuana only because I didn't know anything about it. . . . Danny came home to visit once with his girlfriend, and we were sitting around, and all of a sudden Danny whips out a joint with no embarrassment. I loved it. It was nice. He passed it around, and we all had some—it was like a lovely ceremony. I later found out that Danny was heavily into drugs when he was at Harvard. He told Laura that he tried LSD. I was surprised because he was always such a purist. If I had known about it, I would have tried to talk him out of it because it scared me. I just cared about his welfare. I've never cared what other people thought.

When Danny grew his hair long, everyone was on me about it. Thank God there was the valedictorian who gave the address when Danny graduated from high school. This boy was a decathalon Olympic champion—he was an American hero. And he got up there and said, "I just want to say this on the subject of hair. It doesn't matter how you wear your hair. It's what you have between the ears that counts."

I did feel bad when Danny graduated from Harvard receiving his diploma in a green poncho. He refused to wear the cap and gown. That hurt. It really hurt. I do think that traditions should be observed, and yet I'll admit I don't observe them myself. For example, I was brought up a Catholic, but I took it all with a grain of salt. However, my kids did go to church—we all went. As soon as Laura got married I never went again and my kids aren't religious now.

My daughter didn't like living in Connecticut. It was snobby and cliquish, and she was miserable. We lived six miles out of town in the woods all by ourselves. She was very shy and is to this day. She was very different from me. I tried to build up her confidence. I tried to encourage her to be outgoing. We bought her her own car. She had no curfews, no rules. I encouraged her to bring her friends to the house. I told her that love and good sex makes you beautiful. When she asked me about sex, at first I was really tongue tied. I didn't know what to say. But then I said, "Sex sounds ridiculous, but actually it's fun." And I told her that my first romance was so pleasurable and enjoyable that it put me on the right track forever after. I told her I was very fortunate in having a young man who was so tender and loving. I told her all about it. I shared it with her. And when she had her first lover she said to me, "To you and Dad, Patrick is only a case of acne (which he did have) on two legs. But to me his body is beautiful and wonderful."

She went off to college and came home for vacations and she said, "Mom, I have to get some contraceptives." And I said, "Really?" And she said, "Yes, I worry so each month. Sometimes I worry so much I can't get my assignments done." So I said, "O.K. We'll visit Dr. Reilly." She said, "Oh, would you take me?" She was too shy to do it. I was so glad she confided in me. I called Dr. Reilly and took her there and sat in the waiting room while he spoke to her privately and wrote her a prescription for oral contraceptives. She called me up once and said, "Mommy, Mommy, guess what? There's this guy, and he's so good looking, and he's so tall, and he asked me to go out with him!" She was so excited. So you see I considered her to be my best girlfriend as well as my daughter. One summer she said to me, "Would you teach me how to cook?" And I said, "That sounds like a lovely project for the summer." And she bought a notebook, and I taught her how to make all the things she liked to eat.

My children had a privileged upbringing, I'll admit. They didn't have to work summers though Danny did deliver papers and do some gardening. Laura went to summer school one summer to study Spanish just to have something to do. The kids belonged to our yacht club. I never made them do anything or forbid them to do anything. I said, "You are students, and as students I want you to concentrate on schoolwork. I didn't have you children to be little slaves around the house. You are not house servants." And they both did fantastically in school. Both were national merit scholars. Both were musical. Danny had a band, and Laura took flute lessons and played in the high school band.

Both of my children are married, and both are doing well. I enjoyed their company when they were young, and I still enjoy their company now. And while we live in different parts of the country, we all visit back and forth quite often and I still consider them my best friends.

RACHEL

"I wasn't going to help Adrienne by being miserable. Whatever had happened in the past had happened, and it could be mended. It wasn't irreparable."

Rachel teaches elementary school. Her ex-husband is a university professor. They are gentle, intelligent, reasonable people who paid a lot of loving attention to their two daughters. But just as the girls became teenagers their pleasant family life was disrupted. Rachel and Matthew decided to separate largely because Rachel had finally acknowledged to herself, and to her husband and daughters, that she was a lesbian.

Rachel, though philosophically and psychologically sophisticated, was "thrown" by her oldest daughters extreme, though understandable, reactions to the family turmoil. Rachel was wise enough to enlist the help of others—a professional therapist, guidance counselors, her best friend Jane. She was able to listen to them and act on their advice. She realized that she must let Adrienne go, let her express herself, and not give in to her instinct to overprotect her. She managed to do this with compassion and understanding always reassuring Adrienne with love and concern.

Hannah was thirteen, Adrienne was sixteen when Matthew and I separated. They reacted differently because they are so different. It was more difficult for Adrienne, my older daughter, because she has a lot of anxiety. It is just her temperament. Anyway, for us to break up caused her a lot of anxiety.

She had been sick; she'd had mononucleosis, and she was out of school during that time when we were thinking of separating. Then she became well, but she refused to go back to school. What happened was she wouldn't leave the house. Matthew and I were getting some counseling at the time, and I talked to the counselor about it, and she said it was possible that Adrienne thought if she didn't leave the house, our marriage wouldn't fall aprt. We finally got a tutor. Then we arranged with the guidance counselor to let her go to one class one week, then two the next. We did it slowly. Her school phobia was a problem for about two years.

Eventually she saw a therapist, but she resisted that for a while. She needed a lot of attention from me, and I was not giving it to her because I was in the process of forming a new relationship. Not going to school was her way of saying: "Hey, here I am, and I'm having a hard time and you'd better help me out." I began to realize that she needed some attention.

At the same time that Matthew and I separated I told the girls I was a lesbian. That also caused Adrienne more anxiety than Hannah. She was angry at me and angry at Matthew, and she was scared. She began going to counseling then, but she wouldn't talk about sexual problems for almost a year. Her counselor finally said, "You have to confront the nitty gritty of the situation. Don't come back unless you're willing to discuss this." It was difficult for Adrienne, but she went back and began to talk about it. That was just before she went to college. Her going to college, making a break with me, was a severe problem for about six months. Adrienne and I were pretty dependent on each other even though we hadn't been getting along well. We needed each other, and yet we were better off without each other.

She came home for a visit after two weeks, and we had a fight, and she said, "Fuck you." and left the house. As she was leaving I screamed at her, "I know you have to do this, and I wish the hell I had done this when I was your age." It came back to me, the same kinds of feelings I had when I was eighteen, but I never would have done what she was doing.

She kept in contact with people here. She called Jane. So for months Jane was her friend and her therapist. Since Jane is my closest friend, I felt tremendously relieved that she had someone to talk to because I knew she really needed it. But I also felt jealous because she could trust and talk to someone else, but not to me, although I understood why. I wanted to know how she was, but I didn't want to know the details. I just wanted to know she was o.k.

I wrote to her and told her she could come home anytime. In the beginning I was angry and upset, and I was sorry for myself. I would go for long walks and think, "My life is really too screwed up. . . . I don't want to live. . . . It's irreparable." But then I began to realize from talking to Jane that Adrienne was having a much harder time than I was, and that I should stop feeling sorry for myself. I wasn't going to help Adrienne by being miserable. Whatever had happened in the past had happened, and it could be mended. It wasn't irreparable. So I wrote her and said, "I know you're going through hell, but whenever you want to come home it's fine."

I didn't feel so guilty anymore. I didn't feel like destroying myself because of my horrendousness. It was an enlightenment for me as well as for her. She did come home, and we sat in the living room, and she said, "I'd like to talk." We started talking about one in the afternoon, and I remember it got dark, and we sat there with the lights out talking till nightime. She asked me all the questions she had on her mind. At the end she said, "I think I'm a lesbian." And we talked about that. Then she said, "We might not talk like this for a long time because we have to keep some distance. I see I can make it on my own. I don't need you to survive." And I said, "And I don't need you to survive." It was marvelous. It was an incredible thing. Then we hugged. And we didn't talk for a long time afterwards, but we didn't fight either. We did not want to be close friends—we wanted to be mother and daughter.

My life was mine, and hers was hers. It's not that we kept secrets, but we didn't confide in each other.

When she came to visit on vacations, we laughed a lot, and we had fun. I actually looked forward to it. She was no longer so angry with me. It wasn't, "Look what's happened you're a dyke and now I have to be a dyke." It was "Hey, this is a way of life for me, and I'm excited about it." She considers herself gay. She's active in gay organizations, and has had one serious relationship with a woman. Adrienne also has a lot of male friends.

I feel like she's another adult. It's so equal now. We still argue, we still have problems, but I can say things to her without hurting her feelings. She still calls and says, "Can you send me some money?" But I can say, "Yes, I can." or, "No, I can't right now, can you wait a few weeks?" And I don't feel guilty. But in order to have this happen she had to break contact. But of course, through all of this, she did have Jane.

And there were, of course, what she calls "breakdowns." The spring after we talked, she called and said, "I haven't slept or eaten for a week." My instinct was to get in the car and go get her, but I called her therapist and said, "This is what's happening." And her therapist said, "If you go get her, she's never going to know that she can take care of herself. This is a test for her. She hasn't slept, she hasn't eaten, and she is in bad shape. But you don't have to go get her. She isn't going to die." And I asked her, "Is she going to hurt herself?" The therapist said, "I don't know that. I can't tell you that she's not going to, but my guess is that she isn't."

So I called her and said, "Give it one more day. Try to sleep. Go to the infirmary and get some sleeping pills. Try to eat something and call me tomorrow at this time. And if you still haven't had any sleep and still haven't eaten, I will come." And yet I wanted to go immediately. But she called me the next day and said, "I slept. But I'd like to come home this weekend." And I said, "Fine." She went through almost a whole other week after that before she came home. She was feeling terrific because she had done it.

I feel free to love her again now. It's so easy to love her. Before I was feeling guilt. I was feeling insecure about being gay myself. Now I see it's o.k. to be gay, and I don't worry about it, and I don't worry about her at all. I think about her, but I don't worry about her. It's nice to see her feeling good about herself. I'll admit I overprotected Adrienne to the point that she didn't know she was competent. It took us a long time to overcome this but, finally, we did.

JESSICA

"Some people might consider Gabriel and me failures because Gabriel's gay. They would overlook all his other attributes; the fact that he was gay would ruin everything. For me, Gabriel is the perfect son."

Jessica, an unconventional and colorful woman, is perhaps a new age "hippie" on the surface and an old-fashioned matriarch at heart. Attractive, verbal, and highly dramatic, she has long red hair and a rose tattoo on her chest. Confined and restless in a middle class existence, bored by college and vowing to have a child by twenty and at forty, she married an equally unconventional twenty year old and set up housekeeping with him, her new baby Gabriel, and her younger brother.

Her husband left when Gabriel was twelve. Faced with debts and no child support, she worked at odd jobs and managed to provide a stable home and loving care for both her son and her brother. In spite of limited resources and an unconventional nomadic lifestyle, Jessica did provide Gabriel with the best of everything—interesting adult friends, a rich social life, and a superior education.

Jessica is now a mother again at forty-one. Gabriel will graduate this year at the top of his class from a prestigious eastern college. He has always been a high achiever, is well liked by everybody, and is a thoughtful and perceptive young man. It is obvious that Jessica and Gabriel have had a warm, nurturing, and mutually respectful relationship.

Gabriel has always been an incredibly good student, has always gotten straight A's, and been very well liked by his teachers and his peers. He's very popular, a real leader. He's been student leader, student president, student everything. He's interested in languages and good at them; he's fluent in Spanish and in Arabic and speaks a little Persian as well. He loves to write and has won awards for Creative Writing. He's just good at everything. And he isn't—and I feel good about this—a genius. Some people like to think that Gabriel has some incredible I.Q. I don't believe he does. I think he's very bright and he has good study habits. I taught him how to study. I was a good student myself, a high achiever.

I sent him to boarding school after his first year in public high school, not because he was doing poorly in public school but because I saw him getting bored. He was getting all A's and accolades and awards, and I didn't see him doing much for it. He wasn't interested in his work. I would ask him about it, and he'd have nothing to say. I would go to his teachers, and they would rave about what a fine young man he was, how handsome, how mannerly. True, but what was he learning?

I was raising him alone. There was a lot of loud music, smoking dope, hanging out. The neighbors were complaining; the police came a couple of times. It was just too much for me. I was trying to work and keep my life together, and all these kids were around all the time. I didn't fear anything terrible happening, the kids were all really nice. I just feared he was wasting his time. And his education was definitely mediocre.

So he went to boarding school in his sophomore year and did well there. The first semester was hard for him. He was lonely. and he had to work very hard to get his grades. Of course, he only got one B, the only B he's ever gotten, but he was putting himself under a lot of pressure. He was tense and insecure. He didn't like his roommate. He now says that it was the worst time of his life. But it soon turned into the best.

I went to private school also, and I was miserable the first semester. I told him, "Once you get into it, when you go back after Christmas, all of a sudden it will start to click. It will feel like home, the work will get easier, and it will be the best time of your life. I guarantee it." I also helped him to change dorms and get a more appropriate roommate. And things did get better. He became a student leader, spent a semester studying in Spain, was salutatorian of his class, and again won many awards.

One of the reasons I was successful with Gabriel is that we are very similar personality types. So I am able to say with some sureness, "I know best." I can tell him what he will enjoy, and I'm seldom wrong. So I was able to say about him going away to school, "I know you are going to love it. It's going to be good. I guarantee it." However, he also went to college at Princeton, at my urging, and he does *not* completely love it. That was a slight error.

I thought Princeton would be just his cup of tea. He used to be much more conservative, just like I was in prep school. I should have realized how much he is like me and that he would change and become a little too radical for Princeton. It wasn't a disastrous error; he's doing brilliantly and has made interesting good friends; it just isn't the absolute best. I think he would have been better off at Columbia University, some place in a big city. Because he was also growing into his identity as a gay man—and Princeton's pretty restrictive and limited. But he got all kinds of grants to study in the Middle East during his Junior year, and he loved it. Now he's shooting for a Fulbright, hopes to go back there for a year, and then maybe to law school. Gabriel, as his Grandmother puts it, is going to be able to write his own ticket because he is very accomplished and very personable.

I did instill definite values in Gabriel. I was very fussy about manners, appearance, grades. These things I now think are a bit of bull-shit, and I don't respect them quite as much any more. But the good thing he learned from me—and his father—is to be truly a tolerant and humanistic person. He never saw us deliberately hurt other people. He saw us being kind to everybody and not condescending. And he learned by example. I am really a "gentleman," and so is my former husband, and my brother, who Gabriel idolizes. I think Gabriel gained his social graces, his tact, his diplomacy, his sincere interest in others from us and also his way of drawing other people out. He's really gifted at that.

Another thing that was helpful in a strange way is that we were in a very bad economic state, so he had to work hard, and he had to achieve. We were very poor, scraping along at the bottom. So there wasn't any choice for Gabriel. He couldn't just sit and smoke dope and party. He wasn't spoiled, not because I wouldn't have spoiled him if I could have, but fortunately, I couldn't. So Gabriel has worked since he was fourteen. He had to. I had no money. In a way, I think it's easier to raise kids when there is no choice. Maybe it goes more smoothly when you simply must live in a small space as we did. We absolutely had to share household chores. There was just no question. I did, of course, have my problems with the chore list. That was an ongoing problem. I had to crack the whip around the house, and believe me I did. Gabriel and his uncle (my brother who lived with us) often called me Herr Commandant.

I *was* extremely vigilant and involved. By some people's standards, I certainly wasn't a strict mother. I allowed him to smoke dope, to wear bizarre clothes, to say "bad words," but I always knew what he was doing. I oversaw everything, from the kind of underwear he wore on up. I pried into everything he did. Too much maybe.

But I do think vigilance is important. And although my rules were kept to an absolute minimum, mostly rules of consideration—calling when you're going to be late, helping out around the house—they were enforced. I've watched friends with kids just like my own, bright, attractive, energetic, become monsters because their parents were too lax with them and didn't follow through. The few times Gabriel did disobey me, I went after him. Literally. I dragged him out of a movie I had forbidden him to see by his hair. I called the police one night when he didn't call in. And I would order him home from friends' houses if he hadn't cleaned his room properly.

It's a mystery to me how one does gain one's children's respect. I've seen people tell their kids what to do, and the kids just don't do it. I don't know what I would have done if that happened. But I was demanding from the start so he knew what was expected. Eventually, I relaxed a bit. But it's easier to start out demanding than to try to reverse the process. And as I said, I was only strict about little things, never about whom he slept with or anything like that.

Perhaps some of this has contributed to his homosexuality. I don't believe that Gabriel is a "new model" homosexual. The new model is that people are just born that way, and that homosexuality has nothing to do with the father or mother. I think in Gabriel's case, it had a lot to do with an over-protective, overbearing mother, but even more to do with an absent father. I think he's still searching for a man who will love him. And Gabriel blames me a little too. He once accused me of trying to make him exactly like me. He was looking at some photographs recently and was horrified to see that we were dressed alike a lot. He was the center of my life; I had very little interest in anything outside of him, my brother, and our survival. He also saw my ex-husband mistreating me a lot, saying terrible things to me, getting me very upset. Gabriel definitely identified with me, sided with me; he was very protective and worried about me. I once asked him if he ever wanted me to get married again, and he said absolutely not. He never wanted another man around the house again. I think he knew too much about my life, my straits. That gave him an anxiety level I'm not too happy about. But it also turned him into a sensitive, caring, dutiful son.

I had a few fights with Gabriel when he was going through his conservative phase, the early teenage years. He was embarrassed to bring friends to the house. It was small and funky. I was walking around with my tattoo in various stages of undress. I knew he wasn't finding me acceptable because I wasn't straight enough. One night he said he wanted to invite a friend for the weekend, but I would have to hide my tattoo, wear something nice, make something American and non-vegetarian for dinner. He also told me he was embarrassed by our house and the fact that there was no man around and that he had no father. I was on my way to work all night at the bar, a job I hated. So I flipped out, and we had a gigantic, scream-ing fight. I screeched that he was a selfish brat. "How do you think it is for me? Do you think *I* enjoy living in this wretched house with no money, no lover, no husband to take care of me? How dare you say this to me?" I was crying, and he was crying. And I went off to work because I had to.

Something else I should bring up in relation to this that is very important is that Gabriel and I often lived with, or close to, other people. There were other people, specifically my brother and other women around for him to talk to. And this is what saved the day this time. A good woman friend of mine happened to drop in after I had left for work, and Gabriel was sitting there sobbing. They had a long discussion about it, and he called me up at work and apologized. When I got home I said, "I'll tell you what. Invite Jimmy over, I'll make spaghetti and wear clothes, but I guarantee you (my usual!) that this will be the coolest place he has ever been in his life. He will love me, and he will love this house." Well, Jim was a very straight kid who lived in a trailer, and he did love it. My point was proven. Slowly Gabriel learned to utilize my eccentricity and bohemian existence to his advantage. He became very popular. Everybody wanted to come to our house. Then he got his ear pierced, let his hair grow, and got a lot of attention in his own right. This was in the sixties when it was fashion-able to look bizarre. He did well with it. He can still turn it on. It's fun to be bizarre sometimes.

So, as you can see, he was a good teenager, no trouble with drinking or dope, though frankly I don't know why not, since

I always allowed him to do it. I wonder now, could I have stopped it if I saw it getting out of hand? I guess I could have because for some reason Gabriel has always been afraid of me. But I don't think, in retrospect, that I would advise anyone to be as permissive about drugs as I was. I also think it would have been healthier if he lashed out at me a little more than he did. I remember once he told me he hated me, and I flew into a rage. I said, "You may never say that to me. You can go write it down, you can sit and think it, you can plot my death, but you can never say that to me." I was so exhausted and harassed by my life I couldn't take him saying that, but now I hope I'd have the maturity to understand it.

I also wish I had shown my love for him more directly. My brother, my son, and I are all good sociological observers. We make fun of everything and everybody, including ourselves. Our interaction within our little family was largely based on teasing and putting each other down—in a loving way of course. But I think we did it too much. As a result, Gabriel tends to be a little too cool, a little too detached and analytical.

Right now, it's hard for me to predict what will happen to my Gabriel, what he will become. I used to think he would be President, then I decided that Secretary of State would be better. Not too grandiose! But perfectly attainable and probable for Gabriel. Now he tells me that he won't be Secretary of State because he doesn't like the people in the State Department. I've always thought that Gabriel would be a high-earning, establishment-facade, person. He would have a conservative life-style and then underneath would be his own unique and liberal soul. And of course, he would have a wonderful relationship with a good, strong person . . . man . . . woman. . . . Now I'm not so sure. He'll most likely make money because he loves money, but he may not be Secretary of State or even a lawyer. He's going to go more to the left than I thought. And I'm glad.

Some people might consider Gabriel and me failures because Gabriel's gay. They would overlook all his other attributes; the fact that he was gay would ruin everything. I don't care at all about that. I find it interesting and intriguing. It's not important to me. For me, Gabriel is the perfect son. He has been, and continues to be, the joy of my life and my proudest accomplishment.

MOLLY

"Clarity is what I would say is needed between parents and children. Letting kids know who you are, what you value, what you want at a given moment as best a parent can. . . . The more clarity the better."

Molly is a linguist, a teacher, who has traveled throughout Europe and parts of the Americas. She has raised one son, mostly on her own, due to the fact that she became a widow at an early age. She grew up in the years she raised her son, always aiming at becoming more "together." Although money was hard to come by, she did hustle and managed to keep the home going as well as save for a few trips and private schools for her son. She had problems with ambivalence, not knowing what she stood for, what her values were, who she was, but she was not afraid to seek help. Throughout she has tried to grow personally and is what might be called a self-actualizing person.

Did I have any problems with my teenager? Yes, I had problems. My son Richard was seriously, heavily into drugs—marijuana mostly, and liquor as well. This scared me because his grandfather is an alcoholic. I also had problems because he had been a very docile, easy child. As a teenager he became mischievous, showing a "villainous" side. He became nonproductive. Prior to that he had been involved in piano and computer science, both of which he excelled at.

Then the adolescent stage: he would sit around and smoke dope, and he had serious personal problems to work out.

They stemmed from his own family life (a semi-extended as well as single-parent situation) and from the fact of his father's death during Richard's infancy. According to one of the psychologists, he saw the act of separation, because of his father's death, as frightening. Any separation was traumatic, and yet he knew and wanted separation from his only remaining parent, in this case, me, his mother. He was clearly aware of the memory of the time prior to his eighteenth month when his father died. He remembered a happy time in contrast to what followed: a drab, grey unhappiness on the part of his parent. Many ensuing years of financial difficulties as well as his parent's struggle to find herself and get on her own two feet. During the "happy time" he had already begun speaking one language (we lived in Europe), and then we moved back to the States to my parents' home (a home of alcoholism and many other personal problems and idiosyncracies). Here he stopped speaking for a long time until, in about his third year, he started talking English. The contrast was great from one place to the other due also to the fact that we had been in a touchy-feely country, so to speak, where there was much warmth among people, friends, family members; and now we found ourselves in a home of rigid, undeveloped feelings. Each of the members of this latter household have, over the years, made their own attempts to become more demonstrative and feeling.

As to other problems? Well, I was the only person in the household (after we moved away from my parents' home, having stayed with them four years). The problem here was closeness. He and I did many things together, he went almost wherever I went. This was the result of the small family structure, also lack of money for babysitters, and my own insecurities too.

The whole process of his growth as a teenager, his violent breaking away—all of this seemed like a rotten process but which in the long run was a healthy one. He wanted separation. As I mentioned before it was a trauma for him. But "you're no longer mine and I'm no longer yours" was his feeling and "dammit I'm going to go out and make my own mark in this world without you!" (Here came "trauma" and sorrow for me, of course, because his violence hurt; I was afraid of the changes—there always seemed to be so many, including my own development.) But he did spend several adolescent years separating and was highly abusive towards me, and here we are today at which point he is back to being very productive, is engaged, and we are getting along very nicely. Our relationship seems to be wholesome and communicative.

In his adolescence, though, our relationship no longer held any sharing. There was no warmth in the house. Of course, I had gone through a whole evolution myself. And in many ways *I* was the one who had done a whole separation from him. Slowly of course; it was a process which was more or less completing itself at the time he began his rowdy rebellion. I also married someone for a short time. This was a fiasco, and it confused my whole relationship with Richard. But, both the marriage and my own growth, although they were threatening to him, were healthy challenges. They made him begin to know the outer world a bit more.

Our communication in some ways had been good. We had many good times together. And yet, I often would "listen" and not really listen. I was preoccupied, unable to concentrate on the moment. And of course he picked that up. I was busy earning money, trying to live a decent, ordered life. I wanted to survive emotionally, as well. In those years I often wouldn't show my feelings to Richard. If something occurred which would make a normal, flowing person mad, I would often have no feelings I was conscious of, and he picked that up too. "Are you mad?" he would ask. "No," I would hedge ambivalently, not yet able to know my own feelings.

Now we fight it out. There have been many altercations. We are a lot more honest. I used to be afraid of rejection by anybody for showing my feelings. I learned that my own son needed me. He seemed like he wanted to reject me, but he really needed me. Richard's involvement with a psychologist helped him learn to communicate along with my learning to do the same.

In spite of my tenseness and lack of physical demonstrativeness, there was a certain exposure Richard did get to many types of people, to different interests, culture, sports; there was also his knowledge that, no matter what, I really did love . . . adore . . . my kid and that I had the patience to stick it out during his extremely difficult adolescence.

I began to learn how to "say it like it is" and take life more as it is in the here and now and that helped him. Before, my ambivalent messages confused him. Clarity is what I would say is needed for good relations between parents and children. Letting kids know who you are, what you value, what you want at a given moment as best a parent can. The more clarity the better.

Structure: this is important to a point. I had learned structure in my early years, and some of this I carried over into my adult life. His meals were regular. I was a hard worker. In many ways I was very laissez faire, and if I were to re-raise him I would be a *tiny bit* less so, but basically the same. There were some things I would do differently. For example, I demanded little of him by way of chores. It was easier for me to do everything myself rather than go through the process of getting someone else to do it. And since kids don't always want to do their duties, they end up taking time, and time and energy were things I didn't always have a lot of. There was one kind of structure which I remember demanding and which he followed almost perfectly: that of reporting to me if he changed location, if he were in places such as around a swimming pool or at the ocean, etc. Having structure when needed is important.

My unstructured way of exposing him to piano lessons allowed him to pick and choose for himself. He had his first few violin lessons, and simultaneously he wanted to have piano lessons. "O.K.," I said, figuring that one or none, or maybe even both would "take." At any rate, the violin was dropped very soon, and Richard did very well in piano. This is laissez faire, but it worked for me. I know some parents wouldn't be comfortable with that.

In an area that many parents are comfortable—that of demanding their children be top students—I was extremely ill at ease. I was permissive, laissez faire again about this. At times he knew I wanted him to do better, but perhaps because I disliked much of my studying and was an out of school experimenter, I felt it was o.k. to be permissive. Richard has one or two credits to go to finish high school which he left two years ago. He seems to be the type who will get his education when he needs it and/or wants it. He is now improving himself in his self-taught field of the guitar by taking lessons. I did send him to boarding school because I thought this would help encourage academic interests. Although he had once been a good student, he was not so in boarding school. However, he benefitted socially in the long run from this investment. Also, it was a structure other than his own home, and I felt this would work better than constantly exposing him to me whom he was trying to separate from.

If I had it all to do over, there is one item I would control: the TV. Richard ended up with problems in separating TV life from real life. Not only violence on TV but Brady Bunch family life, perhaps; or the way people relate on TV as opposed to the infinite number of ways people can relate in reality. I used the TV as a babysitter often. Never again. Only good entertainment. I don't think the TV should be a substitute for out of doors, for people, for hobbies and interests. He is now a discriminating viewer.

Richard's development is exciting to me. He seems steady. I like what I see in his desire to relate to people. I like what I see in his relationship to his fiancée. They seem to be a normal couple, who don't abuse drugs and liquor. They like to work and play and party sometimes. Richard's self-destructiveness of recent years has vanished. His trouble with the police (he burglarized a store with other fellows and then was involved in vandalism) . . . this trouble was also, in a way, healthy. He wanted attention. He wanted help. He wanted family members (including grandparents) to rally around and prove their love.

My patience was worn. But I *was* patient. The intensity of his rebellion was so painful to me, I often wanted out, but his psychologist kept reminding me how it was important to follow through, to keep showing my son that I cared. Great advice, because I was not at all in touch with this. I needed to be educated to so many things, especially that of a teenager's saying, "I hate you, go away, you're a terrible parent." I responded so literally, so hurt. But the knowledge coming from someone who saw into Richard helped me. So, I did stick it out. I have always stuck by him, when he needed something; love, money, etc.

He does want to be his own man now. He doesn't want to take advantage by asking for money. He seems to be growing into manhood nicely. He works in a construction business and is often out of doors, where he can also be creative.

Some things I can be proud of in raising him as a teenager . . . one thing of course is the simple sticking by him, being there for him. Also, being determined to become my own person. If nothing else he can at least say: "My mother (I like her, I don't—whichever) did set out to know herself, to repair any damages, to become healthy; she is a person; she tries; she cares. She did her job." I'm glad I'm that kind of example.

Richard knows also that I support him basically and love him. I'm proud of this, too. I don't always agree with him. As I said before, we fight it out, argue, get angry and then next day the air has been cleared, and we're o.k. He knows I have opinions, my own life.

Not having my own regular man now—and then—is—and was—difficult. While raising him, and during his adolescence, it was hard because I could have used a helping hand and a strong one occasionally. Then also I could have been less attached to Richard, and he less attached to me.

In spite of the fact that I felt my parents weren't all that healthy emotionally, I did want to frequent them partly because I wanted to work my relationship out with them and partly because I felt an extended family, no matter what kind of hang-ups or difficulties they were having as people, would be of utmost importance to Richard. My parents, as parents to me, were in some ways good: let's say my mother sincerely wanted to be a good mother, but she chose to mother her husband instead; and my father was never around mentally because the major part of his life was spent drunk. When he wasn't drunk it was to meet important—to him—obligations such as choir practice and choral society. Rarely did he try to develop his relationships with his children. Or when he did he seemed to be unaware of the fact that his neglect of his family should cause difficulties in relating after-the-fact. I learned a great deal from him: you can't do anything with your life if you sit around and don't do it! You can't gain respect unless you really earn it! You can't force others to believe in you and go along with all your bad points forever. I learned that if you don't iron out *every* wrinkle, a wrinkle will always be there.

I tried to do things differently from them. I remember thinking, when Richard was a baby: one thing my parents didn't do was enjoy their children. There was conflict, constant hatred, little joy. I wanted and was going to enjoy my child. Not to be like my parents in many ways was important. For example, I didn't want to ogle over things, people, family background like my parents did. I didn't want to live beyond my means as my parents had done. I wanted a good relationship with my child. Easier said than done of course because if one is brought up a certain way one's personality is enmeshed in the parents' way of life. I wanted to be stronger than my mother and learn not to blame: my mother blamed the alcoholism for her pain. But she chose daily to stay, and even to hide behind her husband's alcoholism. I wanted to make something of myself.

Both my son and myself see the "flaw"—so we call it—in my parents. They were spoiled, sheltered, rich kids, adults who met and married and met some measure of hell along the way together. Both of us admire work, doing, activity, finding out what's really what, living life as it is, as it comes. . . .

Richard's evolution, his process, seemed negative, but it led to good. It all began when he was born! He made it through his difficulties—father's death, mother's being out-of-touch and desperately fighting to come alive—because of, I think, an enormous love I felt for him. I know he knew that he was a loved child.

The fact that his growth has brought him back to life, back to me in a way that I can enjoy (and I think he can too) is of course very exciting. The fact that he has come out of his difficult period and is now relating to an individual he lives with and is planning to marry is marvelous. I don't experience jealousy, though at times I have felt a third-wheelishness. And when the three generations spent the past summer together in my parents' house—I in between my father and mother and my son and future daughter-in-law—there were moments when I felt a bit out of sorts, out of place. Of course, being located between the two generations and single, it is natural to feel at times just plain different.

I am particularly pleased when I see that Richard has become a very tactile person, touchy-feely with his fiancée and even others, myself included. This is part of his will to be a feeling person, a person who lives life fully. I'm thrilled he has this relationship for many reasons: 1) it frees me a bit; 2) it gives him great pleasure; 3) it keeps him steady and in good company (and therefore not in bad company, i.e. roaming the streets, prone to trouble with the police and macho competition); 4) he has something to work for together with his mate.

Basically I attribute Richard's pulling out of his serious emotional problems and confusion to the fact that he knew there was strong love and emotional backing and great patience. I'm ignoring heredity of course. He seems to have inherited strength and sensitivity. He knew also that the patience was not to last forever. He knew that I was finally coming to a point of no return. I think he was also aware I loved his father and his father's family. I would take him to visit my in-laws occasionally. He knew that progress could occur through work. I think he saw this in my own liberation. Even though there was often little money and I was often grumbling, bemoaning that fact, Richard knew that I would find a way. Perhaps he learned that where there's a will there really is a way.

If you have a problem to figure out just start doing something. Keep weeding out the wrong answers till you see what the right ones are. Other values he must have picked up: the importance of parenting, the importance of giving. In a way I had sort of Christian values, and I learned that my energy wouldn't give out. I could just keep on going. This is something my parents didn't seem to have. I think my son saw someone who began to learn to harness the energy within. He knows I want to keep growing. And he seems to be going very much in that direction. I feel secure about his desire for a good life.

FLORENCE

"I don't think there's any excuse for bringing up children who are a pain; who are a nuisance to society. . . . There's stress to be put on manners which a lot of young parents pooh-pooh."

Florence is an elegant, articulate woman of seventy who looks and acts twenty years younger. Her daughters were raised in an affluent New Jersey suburb. Her husband, Lou, who died ten years ago of a heart attack was a well-known bio-chemist who was often preoccupied with his work. Essentially, Florence took total charge of the children.

Her problems with her two daughters were as dissimilar as the girls themselves. Sara was high strung, high-spirited, energetic and rebellious. Jill was delicate, quiet, and lived under the shadow of a life threatening illness. Today, both girls have their own families and are still dissimilar in personalities but lead equally interesting lives. Jill is a farmer and ceramicist on the West Coast who climbs mountains, skis, keeps bees, and plans to emigrate to New Zealand. Sara lives in a big eastern city, runs her own business, is a talented working painter and moves in chic and sophisticated circles. Florence is proud of them both, and they are both devoted to her.

Jill's illness was called nephrosis. There was no known cure or treatment at the time because no one knew what to do about it. We went mad and were frantic. It lasted for quite a number of years. We had to have a home teacher that the Board of

Education provided called, technically, bedside teaching. Of course, there were many doctors and hospitals and all that.

Her father, being a scientist, would go to the city's libraries and read up for himself since no one knew how to explain it properly, and it wasn't the greatest day of our lives when he came home and announced it was eighty-five percent fatal. We felt quite helpless until the advent of cortisone, and that helped things a lot. Fortunately my brother worked at Merck & Co., and they were the first ones to synthesize cortisone, and he was able to get it for us on an experimental basis—and that really did help because it brought about a remission—it wasn't a cure, but for a number of months things were more or less normal. Then it would start up again. But at least it gave you a chance to catch your breath.

This lasted for at least five years. Then she was able to go to school. But of course then there were other problems, social problems, in that she had not had the experience of other kids, didn't know the social life, how to make friends. But she did well. And I must say, one of the hardest things I had to do was to try to treat her as if she were perfectly normal. In other words, I tried hard not to indulge her and make her feel like an invalid, although she darn well knew that she was, and I knew it too.

I did take to heart one little suggestion that a pediatrician made, and he said, "Remember, try to treat her as if she were a normal child because if you don't, this condition may go away, and you'll be left with something just as bad or worse." And I never forgot that. And, in doing so, I had to battle her grandmother, her father, all of my friends and neighbors who looked upon me as if I were a tough nut with two heads because I didn't flutter about and didn't over-indulge her and pat her on the head and make her into a whining little creep because I didn't think she would thank me for that later.

And I must say, I was fortunate because in this case, her illness made her better and stronger than she might have been otherwise. You know she wanted to be a horseback rider—not just a rider but she had to be a jumper.

I didn't stand in her way. I was a bit nervous about it. I would have preferred just English saddle riding but no, she had to ride hunter seat; that meant the high fences and all that. But in a way, I knew she needed to do it. She had something to prove to herself. Then, when she grew older, she had to climb to the top of Mt. Ranier and the blessed Mt. St. Helena which we now all know. She also did yoga and was very good at it.

She did all this, in part, to prove that she wasn't an invalid. But it was also good physical exercise along with the mental discipline. I'm sure it was good for her. Of course, I had to hold my breath lots of times and felt nervous about the things she was doing, but I tried not to stand in her way. And I think she's grown up to be a good, strong, straight-thinking person.

She isn't dependent on me at all. That's another thing I always kept in mind. I always felt that as a parent one of my primary duties was to bring up children who could be independent people. When they were infants and little children, I felt it was a mother's duty to oversee very carefully their physical safety and cleanliness and health. But when they grew to be older, I didn't honor any complaints and whining.

Kids always have something to complain about, even if it's only wanting their own way about something. Incidentally, I always tried to say yes if I thought it was a reasonable request. I tried not to say no, but occasionally there arose a situation when I simply had to say no, and when I said "No," they knew I meant it.

And no matter how they tried, they couldn't get me to reverse it. Because before I said "No" I tried always to be accomodating, to say "Yes," but when I said no they understood there was no way I could say yes, and that made things rather clear too.

Until children leave home they're not terribly aware of any

separate relationships. You live in the same house, you're part of the same family, you have the same gripes. It wasn't easy because Lou didn't understand the needs and mores of the younger generation—it was too different from what we grew up on. So I found myself being a buffer nine times out of ten.

My husband was a very busy man. He was not often on hand so he got things second hand from me. I buffered. I guess I protected the children in a way in their teens. For example, Sara's interest in doing modern art: I would find myself explaining to Lou that that was what was happening now.

My other daughter, Sara, was not an easy number either. She was a high voltage, high tension girl. She moved fast and was into everything. We had our frictions up until the time she was married.

I have to admit that from the time she was fifteen through let's say nineteen or twenty I found it very difficult to show any understanding of her. I knew she was a highly social soul. I did try to cooperate. If there was permission given for a party and there were going to be fifteen kids, it usually ended up to be fifty. But we managed somehow. We couldn't create a scene right then and there when the house was full of her guests and friends. You would try to explain the next day that this wasn't fair.

I tried to maintain a pretty steady kind of atmosphere. In fact, it was thrown in my face once. About a year after Sara was married she accused me of giving her a false impression of married life. And I asked, "Why do you say that?" She said, "Because I can never remember a time when you and Daddy had a real fight. I always thought that everything went along smoothly, and when Stefan and I had our first fight I figured our marriage was over." And I said, "Good Lord. What a thing to be accused of." We always tried to keep things on an even keel. I don't think that having fights in front of your kids helps them very much. That isn't to say that in the evenings if we had a disagreement that we didn't discuss things, but we never had any real hollering fights in front of the kids; but then we never had that even when they weren't around. I don't think it does anything for a child's sense of security to hear their parents screaming and fighting together.

I strove to give my kids security. I truly did try to understand "where they were at," as the expression goes; that I knew they were living in another era, in another world, and that it was important for them to be at ease with their peers.

Both my daughters were pretty verbal and spoke up. I'm not sure that they told me everything. But from listening and watching I had a pretty good idea of what was important to them. I understood that it was important for them to fit into their peer group rather than mine. And I did try to understand. There were times of course when I blew my top and said, "That's absurd and I think it's ridiculous and no—you may not." But I saved those outbursts for when it was really important. Otherwise you'd find yourself screeching morning, noon and night.

My children were my primary interest in life. I did not go back to work after I became a parent. I was on the scene and that was my job, I felt. I thought they were interesting kids. I was interested in them, and our house was open to their friends, and I enjoyed meeting them though I was very often horrified at some of them. And so they felt free about bringing their friends home. They were always introduced. I demanded a certain modicum of manners. Once or twice I had to forbid certain ones. Some were simply not acceptable—they were bad news.

In the community in which we lived, boys and girls started dating early with personal, individual dates. Sara might have been fourteen and a half when she came home and told me that this boy had given her his pin, some kind of club pin to wear, and had invited her to the movies that weekend. And I said, "Sara, I'm sorry, you must return that pin, and you cannot go to the movies with him." And of course she had an absolute fit, and I had it thrown up to me that "Barbara's mother and Susan's mother and all these other mothers allow their daughters to go out with boys." And I said, "Sara, you're living in this house, and the rule in this house says no you may not go out on private dates. If it's a party, a dance some place, if it's a group event, you may go." Of course, there were tears and temper tantrums. It would have been easier to say yes, but I had to say no.

I think that in rearing children your attitude depends entirely on the kind of person you're dealing with—the personality, the temperaments, their needs. Because what works for one doesn't necessarily work for the next one. You have to get to understand your child and try to work according to their needs. But there comes a time when their needs are not always to be honored. Sometimes they're dangerous, sometimes they're ridiculous.

I also don't think there's any excuse for bringing up children who are a pain; who are a nuisance to society. I still think there's stress to be put on manners which a lot of young parents pooh-pooh. I think they still have to go out into the world and live with other people and get along with them. And I mean *real manners*, not this cocktail party buzzing around. Consideration is what I mean, for others.

ANNE MARIE

"Being home even when I didn't feel like being home . . . caring and giving when I . . . didn't feel like answering one more question . . . driving them places, and disciplining (them) when I didn't even want to."

Anne Marie's story is a painful one—the illness and death of her teenage daughter Rose Anne. But it is also the story of her three other daughters and of Anne Marie herself, and the faith that helped them all to endure.

Anne Marie is a special education teacher living in a small prosperous suburb. She is deeply religious, a strict no-nonsense disciplinarian adamantly opposed to drugs, cigarettes, casual drinking, sexual experimentation. She has always demanded that her daughters do household chores and also work at part time jobs to earn their own money. She raised her children alone, and knew from the start what she wanted from them. She was very firm, very consistent (though she admitted this was difficult), very watchful, even while working four jobs! She also found time to take in a foster child, Holly, who's now in college, but still spends all her holidays with Anne Marie and her family. She was endlessly loving and caring but never afraid to say "No" and mean it. At the same time she allowed them every possible healthful opportunity—travel, music lessons, riding lessons, ski trips because she feels, "The more things you know how to do the more secure you are in this world."

Anne Marie is a woman who has faced the worst fear and triumphed, a woman of tremendous strength and vigor, and apparently her beautiful daughters are as courageous and energetic as she is.

My children: my oldest daughter, who went to Heaven three years ago, was sixteen—she would have been nineteen, or whatever age they are up there. Then Rebecca is seventeen. My Maureen is sixteen, and Sally will be fifteen in November. I had four girls. It was great. I loved it, we're very close together. My oldest daughter Rose Anne was the one who died. She died of a rare disease called Addison's disease. This disease is not always fatal, but my daughter just went into an Addisonian crisis and died in my lap going to the hospital. I am happy that she . . . that God allowed that I would be there because she was a very hard worker.

She worked at the Crossroads Diner after school till ten, eleven o'clock at night. She could have been riding all by her little self home in the car. She was coping with the disease beautifully, better than I was. She was a very strong, self-directed person with a tremendous amount of faith and a lot of zest for life. She was never lazy, never. I think that she was so fabulous, I'm so pleased that she was mine, for that short amount of time. She's such an inspiration to her sisters and to my friends and to everybody who knew her.

When she was in the hospital (one of the things that happens is there's a loss of memory, and this was her Junior year, which is a crisis year anyway in school, and she was taking geometry, I think, a geometry regents, and she was very upset because I put her in the hospital in May), she called up the Board of Education in the City of New York, asked them for a tutor which she got. The tutor came every day. She told the doctor when she was taking the regents. They gave her extra injections intravenously of saline solution and gave her a private room so she could take the regents, and she passed with a seventy-five. And she cried because she wanted a ninety-five.

Her suffering started when she was fourteen and a half. When she came out of the hospital, she lived about nine months after that. She died three years ago, September nineteenth, in the first month of her senior year.

Rose Anne packed every minute. Every minute. She was

happy, hard-working. She knew exactly what she wanted to do in life. She had it all planned out. She was already accepted in college. Her intensity wasn't a result of her disease. She always was very industrious. The only thing that happened afterward, she became very old in that there wasn't that teen-age giggling. She was much more serious about things.

It did take me a long time to get over this. I was very angry at first. I had a hard time. I was very strong at the wake, at the funeral, because there were four hundred people there; and I could not say that here I was, a follower of Christ, a lover of God, falling apart. I do believe that God gives life, and God can take it away, so I couldn't collapse. I was very strong then. Actually, I went through worse times when she was in the hospital because I was teaching all day. I went to the hospital at six o'clock at night. I stayed weekends at a girl friend's apartment, so then I could go back and forth every day and Saturday and Sunday just stay.

Rose Anne was terrific; she put on a bikini and went up to the sun porch. She had long, blond hair; she lost it because of the cortisone so I had a wig made of it. It cost a lot of money because it was shaped nicely. Then she gained a tremendous amount of weight on cortisone. But she still had this feeling about herself that was wonderful. She went up and sunned herself in her bikini. This is between practically dying and then coming back.

She and I would go to mass on Sunday. One time the priest said, "I'd like a volunteer to read." (We have readings from the Old and New Testaments.) She raised her hand, had shorts on, went right up and read. She didn't feel defeated in any way. Then the doctors came and told me they thought she had terminal cancer of the kidney. Since the adrenal glands are on top of the kidney, it looked like the whole kidney. Then it turned out not to be that, and when we found out what it was I said, "You will explain to Rose Anne, and you'll not keep anything from her. You will tell her exactly what is going on, what medication she needs, what tests are going to be taken."

Sometimes I'm not afraid to say anything. I've had a lot of problems with doctors, but these guys were wonderful. Rose Anne was very good, took everything. A week later she went to Bermuda with her grandmother and her father and her sisters. That scared me, but they taught me how to give a needle for an Addisonian crisis. In fact the night she became ill, it just never dawned on me that this was Addisonian crisis. I thought it was a bad asthma attack. Because when the adrenalin is low you get an asthma attack.

I remember once while she was sick getting very drunk at my girlfriend's apartment. I called up my brother and his wife. They were so scared because I was always the strong one. I was screaming on the phone, and they said, my brother said, "Oh we have to go right down now." Because he never saw me like that. But it was a good catharsis in that I finally fell asleep. I was so exhausted. That was a very bad time. I aged considerably at that time.

I checked out her disease. Books said she could live a relatively normal life, that if she married she would have a crisis if she became pregnant. I said, "That's no problem, is it Rose Anne? You'll just have your tubes tied or you'll use birth control, and you'll adopt children. No problem." She accepted, and I accepted. She could see that I was always very tense, yet I still tried to be up.

She was very strong, she'd be sitting up in bed and say, "Hi, Ma, let's do this, let's do that." A remarkable person, a fighter. Never a whiner but really strong. I'm painting her like a saint. She wasn't, but she was courageous. I think that she thought she was going to live because I certainly did. I did have it in the back of my mind that maybe something would happen. I always used to go in every single night and look and every single morning, like one does with a baby.

She would become extremely tired. She was finally back in school and doing extremely well. She had been accepted at a Jesuit college and knew exactly what she wanted to do. She was going to take a business administration course. She was going to graduate at twenty-one. At twenty-three she would own her own travel agency, and at twenty-five she would have owned two. She loved to travel. She spoke Spanish. She would have done extremely well. She had this very positive drive. She could still go out and have a good time and dance and go to the discos. Every Friday night she used to take me out to dinner. Even before she got sick, and she used to say, "Come on, Ma." And off we'd go.

Then one night, she couldn't breathe. I thought it was an asthma attack—I'd had them myself. But it got very bad so I got Rebecca, and we started to drive to the hospital. Rose Anne was between us in the front seat. I was driving eighty-five miles an hour and screaming to Rebecca, "Hold her up!" And she was screaming, "I can't, Ma, I can't!" Then I saw, I knew, and I let her lay her head in my lap, and she died.

When we got to the hospital, they worked on her for an hour, but they couldn't get any brain waves. But they still wanted to hook her up to those machines, and I said, "No! God has called her. Let her go."

Rose Anne's death affected my other girls wonderfully, if I can say that. We have strong faith. I tell them that if there's nothing else in life, we have a very strong belief in God. I brought them up—people might think—to be very strict Catholics. But for a reason. Because they develop this faith. When all else fails, there's only one person to call on. And I don't know what people do, I really don't know, without faith.

Faith: it boils down to nothing that's terribly intellectual. Two months before my daughter died, my brother died. He and I were very close. He was killed in a hit-and-run accident. It was one thing after another. I had lost my mother. My brother was going through a very bad period in his life. And I saw him personally go through a purification process, and I think that our life on this earth is so short that we are meant to live in Heaven. We're just here for a very short time, to live happily as we can, but to live with God eventually. I saw that he went through this. I saw Rose Anne go through a purification process, where she learned the absolute basic lessons in life. They both were purified. I think everyone has to be purified before they go to Heaven.

The father of my children was not much help. I don't know why he wasn't much help. Either he couldn't cope with it or accept it. Very few people can. It's bad enough to be the dying person. But it's almost worse for the living, because you stand and watch, you have to endure it; and then you have to pick up the pieces, for yourself, for your husband if you have one, and for my girls.

The rest of my girls—somebody said to me the other day on the phone, "They, your daughters, every time I see them, they are so happy, they're so involved and they are so assertive." Brave, courageous. They are very hard-working. They all work two jobs in the summer. They all do well in school. Rebecca was just voted President of the Student Council. Maureen is in Denmark for a year as an exchange student. And Sally does very well. I think they are very well-adjusted, reasonably happy kids. They also are very good-looking which, I think, helps. They take after their father. They have blond hair, blue eyes, and they are thin, and they are into sports. And they have loads of friends. Even though I have no one left in my family—everyone died within five years, everybody; they're all gone—I have a lot of friends who are family. I have friends who have been friends for over twenty years. I'm very fortunate as far as friends. It's like an extended family. So my girls have a good relationship with these friends, and they can talk to them.

I brought my kids up mostly alone. I have been separated since Sally was four years old. I was always the stronger, the disciplinarian. I started off knowing exactly how I wanted to raise my children. I don't know how I knew it, I just knew. I taught school since I have been eighteen, and I have been around children a lot. And I knew that you don't wait to discipline a child when he's ten, that you do it in the first year.

You have certain demands that you put on children, depending on their age. There have been fights, of course, and arguments, but nothing monumental.

My philosophy was to be strict, very firm, consistent. It's hard to be. It can drive you crazy to be consistent.

Rose Anne always helped me. Even at five years old. And then as soon as the others grew, she would show them how to do things. So there was always the consistency of putting toys away, or whatever the job was. They always did chores, and they never got paid. They still don't get paid. They were expected to help out. After all, it was their house too. I don't believe in giving them allowances for it. They get no allowances at all. They managed by getting jobs outside the house. When they are twelve years old, they must get a job, and from that point on they bought their own clothes. They babysit, mow lawns, do loads of things. And part of the money they earn goes to me for a college fund. Now they are all working in restaurants. Rebecca worked two jobs in the summer. Another thing, this keeps them very busy, so they have little time to get into trouble.

God forbid they should get into trouble because in our area there are a lot of drugs; cocaine is the big thing. The big argument I've had with Rebecca lately at seventeen is that she wants to have a party with a wine-punch and invite all the cheerleaders. Some of the cheerleaders are ninth graders. I said no. Because if I were the parent, and I found out, I would be furious. I'd also be legally responsible. It's a terrible thing, it's so prevalent, you have to fight against the tide. And my kids said exactly what I used to say to my mother: "Everybody is going." So I said, "Good, get a list. Stand up in front of the class and ask how many kids are going." Of course, they never wanted to do that, and I would always call up to find out where the party was. Especially with Rose Anne.

I did more disciplining with Rose because she was the oldest one. Rose Anne got into trouble a couple of times when she was smoking pot in eighth grade. I was like a maniac. I was working four jobs at the time. So I was very tired, but I still kind of checked in after school. I'd run home, then I'd go to my other jobs, then on the weekends, I'd be working. I was cleaning her room. I had taken in another child to live with us. I always had the door open, which is another philosophy. I don't want my kids ever to see that you turn away people who are in trouble. So, they all came, believe me. We have had ten or twelve people there. But it's allright. If they don't like the food, I say, "Go down to the German Deli." I don't cook for anybody. I said, "If you don't like what's in the refrigerator, that's what we have. Tough."

I was cleaning her room, and my ex-husband had the children, all of them. And I found this pipe. So I got on the phone, and I called him, and I said, "Tell Rose to get on the phone." I said, "I want you home immediately!" And he drove an hour and a half to get them back. And I had a belt, big, thick. And I said, "Get into that house."

Holly was the little girl that I was taking care of, who had terrible, terrible problems but who turned out, thank God, to be beautiful, and I hope I had something to do with that. She's a Junior now in college, stays with us every holiday. She's really a lovely kid. It turns out that Holly, when she was in California, her mother let her smoke pot, believe it or not. Holly thought it was the in thing to do. And then got Rose Anne to do it. Well, I really hit Rose Anne with that belt, all over. And I did something I had said I would never do (I didn't want to bring in the Irish guilt, but I did): I said, "I nursed you at my breast. I gave you the finest foods, I never bought canned foods. They're always fresh. . . . And this is what I get." I was crying. I said, "How could you do this to me?" I was like a crazy woman.

And I said to Holly, "You have five minutes to make up your mind. You want to live in my house; you live under my rules. If not you pack that bag, and I will drive you." She decided to leave. In the meantime, Rose Anne was punished for two months, and she never forgot. She was so angry. But my other children, of course, were right there. They weren't in the room, but they heard. Well, they are petrified to touch anything, even now—I hope. And Rose Anne, when she was in tenth grade, said to me, "Ma, I was so angry with you but I was so glad you did that because I was so scared. I'm glad you found out." I was wondering why she was irritable. But I thought it was eighth grade, the change in hormones. It's too young to smoke pot; they get dizzy. I won't teach a high school kid that comes to class on pot. That's the rule. I said, "I don't care whether you do it after school or if you want to ruin yourself. No way are you going to put your butt in this class-room with those red eyes and you can't even see. And I'm trying to teach you?" No way. Or drinking. But that was really the only time I had to come down heavy on Rose. She said that she did it once or twice after that, but she wasn't really interested in it.

They are allowed to drink on holidays. A couple of times when Rebecca and I have gone out to dinner, I let her have a glass of wine. When we went to Europe, Maureen and I, with the high school, we went to France, it's accepted over there. And she and I had a glass of wine. Just so they know that they don't abuse it. I'm against taking drugs. And smoking ciga-rettes is absolutely forbidden. We've had five people in my family die of cigarette smoking. None of my kids smoke. I don't smoke. I don't mind if people do smoke, but I won't allow my children to smoke. And they don't really want to. They're not really interested in it. Because they're athletic. And it's a waste of money when you think of it.

Basically I've had no really serious problems with them. Their choice of friends is exceptional. Beautiful friends. I love their friends, and they have a nice cross-section. They're very friendly with boys and girls. It's none of this nonsense nowa-days—when I was growing up if you had a boy as a friend, he was a boyfriend. Now, everybody gets together. I'm not too keen on dating. Rebecca went out last night to a movie. I usually don't allow them to go out during the week, but she's such a hard-working kid. She's not really interested in the boy, but he's a new boy who came to the school in the Senior year. He asked Rebecca if she would like to go, and she said yes, so they went to the movies. By and large I don't like dating. They're not really interested in that though. They go out in groups of ten or twelve. I think it's fabulous. They have a nice cross-section in that there are boys and girls—Catholics, Protestants, Jews and non-believers. I don't really care who it is as long as they are well-mannered.

I'm a strict Catholic, but I wouldn't mind inter-marriage. I think marriage is such a delicate relationship, probably the most difficult one, on the face of the earth. And if you meet someone that you really are super-involved with, and love very much, what difference does it make? I don't see the difference. I would marry outside my faith. It might make things easier for them to marry in the faith. But I was married to an Irish Catholic, and it didn't work out.

If you set down rules and you're loving and you're there. . . . I was always there. But I don't want to use the word "sacrifice," I don't like that term. "I sacrificed my life for my children." I did it because I wanted to. There was no sacrifice involved. I wanted to have a much larger family than I have now. I wanted six or eight. However, thank God, I could have children. You have to be firm.

My children were the center of my life, maybe too much so. Right now they are because I don't have anybody else. That doesn't mean that I would push them aside, but my focus would become much wider at this point. I can relax a little because they are really formed. They are young adults. Not that I don't have to keep on eye on them, but I'm much freer now. I can go into the city for a weekend because Rebecca will take care of Sally. Another thing I taught my children to do: by the time they were seven or eight years old, they knew how to do the wash, they knew how to dust, they knew how to use the vacuum, they knew how to iron, they knew how to do simple cooking . . . how to put a hot-dog in a pot of water. I didn't do this because I needed them to learn this or because I was so busy. I did it because I think that the more things you know how to do, the more secure you are in this world. They also took horse-back riding lessons, music lessons, singing lessons, drama, whatever. They know how to sail a boat. I want them to be able to say, "I can do this." Never do I want them to say, "Oh, I can't do it." We never use the word fear. At least I don't. I really have very few fears in this world.

My kids have gone places, wherever I went in the city. We lived in the city for a while, for ten years, and I never felt like a lot of friends of mine, "I can't go because I have the kids." I would hail a cab; we would all go. They went to the zoo. We went to the bathroom in the Pierre. Wherever I wanted to go, they would come. They went to all the museums. Even though they were young, they should still get the feeling of walking into a place that's filled with beauty. So I did a lot with them. We've gone on trips. Their grandmother (my husband's mother) was wonderful to us. Very generous. She took them to California, Bermuda. Every year she took us to Florida. They've come to Puerto Rico with me. They've gone skiing. They're very good skiers. They have the feeling that they can do anything. Which I think is terrific. And they also have that which I didn't have, and I wanted to make sure that they had: a very good sense of themselves.

I grew up thinking that I would pass in a crowd. That I wasn't pretty, that I wasn't ugly, but I wasn't pretty. And only when I met this other man, long after I had separated and divorced, did I finally get the feeling that maybe I was attractive. But they've always had that. I think my mother, when she was brought up . . . I think the old families, I don't know whether it was so much the Irish . . . but you were not to look in the mirrors. It's almost like in the convent. You don't compliment your children because you'll spoil them. I always said, "You're pretty, you're beautiful, you look wonderful!" This is what I do in teaching. I always say that. You get much better results.

Except for Maureen, they are all good in school. She's disabled. She's the exchange student. You could see in her letters that she's disabled in that she doesn't put endings on the end of words. "ed's", "ings" she misspells, but she's such a gorgeous kid. She's looking through her value systems in Denmark. She's only been there since August. She said in her first letter that her host father was so ugly. The third letter came back, and she said, "I really love my host father, he's so kind to me. He has grown so beautiful." And I thought, "OK! she's learned, she's gone beyond the exterior." She said, "I never thought in my whole life I would meet such wonderful, beautiful people. They are very simple. They work in a factory. They've never had any more than six years in school, but they're so generous and loving."

According to other people Maureen is very sexy, first of all. She has a wonderful shape, she has long, blond hair, big blue eyes, but she has a sense of herself and is verbally superior to most people despite having a learning disability, which is just in writing and reading. It's a form of dyslexia. Her perception, not her hearing at all, but when she sees and hears a word, it gets twisted in the brain. And she has been working on it herself. Only the persons themselves can work this out. I cannot work with her very well. I get too hyper, and she would ask me at eleven o'clock at night. But, she's very verbal, very social. She went through all the interviews to be an exchange student and made it very easily.

I think it's a wonderful thing that's happened to her because the others had great success in school, and Maureen never really did. Rebecca applied as an exchange student about three months after Rose Anne died. And she came home and she said, "Ma, I think I'd like to be a rotary exchange student." I said, "Oh, Rebecca, please don't. It's too soon." And she never said another word to me, never complained. I said, "I really could not lose you at this time. I really need you here. It's selfish on my part. Once you get to college, I will let you go your junior year, and I'll make sure I have enough money set aside so you can spend your junior year some place." And then the following year, Maureen decided to apply. I said, "Terrific!" She sailed through it, loves it, is doing great. Some of these letters—it makes you cry when you read them. She always was my most sensitive, brightest child. She has a great love of animals. She's very gentle, kind.

My girls have good relationships with their friends. They are very friendly, and they are very giving and sympathetic. For example, a friend of Sally's called, and it seems that her mother is living with this man—I call him a bum—and he came home drunk. It happens to be his house. And he started beating her up. So the girl called up Sally, and said, "Oh, you know, we have to get out of here." So Sally said, "Hold on a minute, my mother will help you." So I said, "Tell your mother to come over here, we have plenty of room, more beds than we can use, as a temporary shelter." Rebecca will say to me, "So-and-so is very sad, Ma, I'm going to go over and take her out to lunch." I think they emulate and imitate me. I know they do. They may criticize me a bit, but then I see them imitate me.

When I get very angry, I tend to swear. My girls are like me in that way, and I don't like to hear that. I have a short fuse, an Irish temper. If I'm reading, the walls could come tumbling down. That's a very bad habit I have. They will talk to me, I'll be reading something, and I'll say, "Uhhuh?" "Listen to this, Ma." I'll say, "OK, go ahead." I read all the time. I read forty books over the summer, and I'm reading constantly. So I'll say, "Go ahead." And then they'll say—my girlfriends will do this to me—"What did I just say?" I'll say, "What?" That's a very bad habit. But I think that to be loving and kind and never to turn your back on anybody who needs help is very important.

I have become active in an organization called International Cross which is essentially a group of small communities which care for a quarter of a million people, mostly in the Third World, but it has a twofold purpose: to take care of suffering in the community and to take care of Third World countries.

One hundred percent of the money collected goes for fuel or fuel banks around here where all the churches and organizations are involved and for a food pantry; we help the migrant workers here and the elderly at the same time. And funds are also sent to a hospital in northern Kenya with 250,000 refugees. My girls are involved in this, too.

My daughters are by and large as energetic as I am. Almost too active, in too many things. They are constantly in school activities. Sally is on the tennis team, she's on the Student Council, she's Secretary of her class. Rebecca is head of the cheerleaders and is also involved in sports.

It's been hard being home even when sometimes I didn't feel like being home. And caring and giving when sometimes I didn't feel like answering one more question. Or driving them places and disciplining when you don't even want to. A lot of hard work went into raising them, but it was worth it. I'm very proud of my girls.

MEG

"When you try to be their friend that makes you just like they are, and you don't know any more than they do. And that makes them feel very insecure."

Meg has four children, fourteen months apart. Her youngest boy was twelve when her marriage broke up. Meg had been totally subservient to her charismatic husband. She describes herself as the "perfect little woman"—an amusing description since she is six feet tall, holds a full time professional job, and has a magnificent singing voice. But in spite of her accomplishments she lacked any confidence in her ability to raise four teenagers. She fell apart, and so did her kids. Through friends' advice she sought help and got it—from a local woman's group and through private therapy. Slowly she began imposing structure on her chaotic household with wonderful results. Today Meg is relaxed and vibrant. Her children are handsome, healthy, energetic. Best of all, the family is a closeknit unit. Meg has since remarried, and life is serene.

Some of the problems that I had with my kids were of my own creation; like feeling guilty because they just had one parent, that I couldn't give them everything they needed. Somebody would be sitting on the living room couch, and they would say, "Mom, could I have a drink of water, or Mom, could I have some orange juice?" And I'd go get them whatever they wanted and carry it out to them. I wasn't smart enough to feel resentful. I'd always done that for Clinton my ex husband,

and felt how lucky I was to be doing it. I was so unaware that I didn't give them a chance to become aware.

I was not used to telling anybody anything. I was used to obeying Clinton's orders, and so were the kids. I felt like I didn't know anything about raising kids. I always felt Clinton knew best. He was so brilliant—he obviously knew everything. So we started at zero—minus zero. I was so exhausted. I was physically in terrible shape. My energy was at a low ebb. They knew nothing about obeying or consistency or that I knew better than they did. They thought I was just another kid to be told what to do by their father.

There were real physical fights between all of us. It's a miracle nobody's dead. My oldest son Ryan was the most destructive. He would do things like put his fist through the wall or start fights. He was constantly hysterical and talking about killing himself. I was really getting scared. We were all fighting and hammering at each other, and the house was about to literally fall down. And I didn't know how to solve it. All I knew about was following Clinton's directions. The kids were hysterical, and I was hysterical.

But I talked to my friend Lenore. She's an amazing woman. I love her. She said "You can do it. You can really do it." But I needed help. I went to a woman's group, and they pointed out that I was trying to be a madonna. They would say, "Doesn't that bother you when your kids act like that?" And all of a sudden I'd realize, Yes, maybe that does bother me. But I hadn't even thought I was allowed to be bothered. I also went to a therapist who was supposed to be an expert on child raising. I ended up in tears and talking mostly about myself. So that's how I got started in therapy.

The children needed something definite from me, not for me to just be one of the boys. When you try to be their friend that makes you just like they are, and you don't know any more than they do. And that makes them feel very insecure. The more structure that they get the better it is for them because they have to have a chance to form their roots. That's what structure's all about.

But it was hard for me to actually impose the structure. Nobody was used to me doing or saying anything definite. We'd sit down to a meal together, and it was disastrous. Fights would break out, arguments. It was terrible. It was really bad. I had to start with basic little stupid common sense things. I had to decide *I wasn't in this world to wait on them. I was in this world to help them grow up to be mature people, not to keep them babies.* I had to learn to say No. "No, I can't get you a glass of water. You've got a pair of fantastic legs, and your arms also work. There are glasses right in here, and you're most welcome."

I learned to not make it a big emotional thing, to not put guilt on them the way I had it put on me. My mother would always do things and work hard. After a big dinner we'd sit and be talking and she'd get up and start doing the dishes. The deal was we were supposed to feel sorry for her and get up and insist on doing the dishes. And this is what I'd do. My kids were supposed to feel sorry for me and then change around instead of me being the grown up and saying, "Look, this is what I expect."

On each of the kid's sixteenth birthday I sat down and had a long talk with them. We don't have any rites of passage in this culture. So on their sixteenth birthday I would get them a really major gift, and we'd also have a major talk. From that time on they were pretty much in charge of their own lives, of getting themselves to school, of getting their homework done, of deciding how they were going to handle problems. But I also told them that any time they got in a corner and felt they needed to use me, they were welcome to. But from then on I was mostly around to pick up the pieces—if there were any problems I was there. So when they turned eighteen they had already had a couple of years to practice being on their own, but there'd also been some constraints, structure, expectations. They also learned the very important lesson that whatever you do there are results—and that part of life is taking responsibility for your actions. Sometimes it feels good and sometimes it doesn't, but that's the breaks.

My kids and I learned the hard way, but now I enjoy them immensely. I have fun with them. They are so open to each other and to me. Ryan and Barry are living together and doing interesting work. Peter's still living at home. He's a high school senior this year and involved in a million things. Carla is a real catalyst to all of us. I think she is the most courageous and interesting woman I know. They're easy to be with, understanding, caring, and yet so independent and self sufficient. But they had to be given a chance to learn about responsibility. I had to stick to my principles knowing the goal was further away. It takes awhile to get things right. That's the reality of life.

I made definite mistakes, but I didn't stop at that. I had to go on, even when I expected the worst. And I grew up with my kids. As I learned about myself, moved forward myself, I was able to help them do the same.

ESTHER and ALAN

"You run the risk of total alienation if you take dogmatic positions which are so foreign to their peer group and to their surroundings. It would be counter productive to oppose them."

Esther and Alan are professionals—her field is early childhood education, and he is an attorney. They are cultured, intellectuals who acknowledge their bewilderment—even fear—of many modern mores and values. But they also acknowledge that they have learned from their daughters and that they were forced to become a little less formal and theoretical and more realistic as they lived through the adolescence of two lively, intelligent curious young women growing up in a sophisticated milieu. The final result seems to be a blending of worlds; the parents respect the daughters, the daughters have assimilated many of their parents essential values.

ESTHER: My concept of discipline is that it comes from within the person. You don't discipline someone else. It has to be a self-process. So any kind of punishment hurts us more than it hurts them.

We thought that reason was a magical thing, that if somebody only knows the right thing to do, they'll do it. You have to have confidence that they have the judgement not to do things for the wrong reasons—that their reasons will be good in what they decide to do.

ALAN: Also you run the risk of total alienation if you take these dogmatic positions which are so foreign to their peer group and to their surroundings. It would be counter-productive to oppose them.

ESTHER: But we did have conflicts, over telephone usage, for instance. We set time limits. I didn't like them spending so much time on the phone. Another one was money conflicts. The question is, to what extent do you, as the source of funds, be the dictator as to how it is to be spent?

ALAN: They accused us of exerting too much control. But we never withheld things they really wanted.

ESTHER: We subsidized things that they wanted to do and that we approved of—camps, survival trips. We would not have paid for them to go to modeling school. Abby was concerned with popular values: clothes, styles, shopping. She could save her allowance for these things, but I would seldom indulge her myself.

They were not allowed to just "watch" T.V. They could only see specific programs and movies. If they were going out, we were rather specific about when they should be in. We were always very much in touch with them. We weren't comfortable with long mysterious silences.

We insisted on familial responsibilities, like attending family functions, dressing in a certain kind of way, and proper behavior in company. We came together at the dinner table. We ate together and talked about the day. Sometimes there were big explosions, and Abby left the table. But we always had dinner together and on weekends, brunch together.

The girls were very involved with the extended family, very close to Alan's family and to my parents who are now ninety-three. My father is rabid on the subject of intermarriage. He would cut off all connection with them if they don't marry Jews. I don't think they would marry a non-Jew while my parents are alive.

ALAN: But of course, they've never gone with Jewish men!

ESTHER: We were never practicing, but we felt that the girls should have exposure to these things so they could make a choice. So we tried sending them to Sunday School for two years. But because it was not reinforced at home it was non-sense. It was fruitless—we don't even believe in God! But on the other hand, they knew my political feelings, and they went to anti-nuclear and anti-war marches with me.

They tried drugs in college. I'm now told that Nina was into a lot of grass in high school. But generally they feel too good about themselves to be really self destructive, so they don't smoke that much anymore. We didn't smoke grass with them until they were out of their teens.

I never felt comfortable imposing my goals head on. It had to be by reason and example. We tried to make our goals for them attractive. I was loathe to impose my expectations on them. I wanted them to come to them themselves. We shared a lot of love and affection, and there was a healthy amount of wanting to please us. I counted on this as a parent. In retro-spect, maybe I should have been less hesitant to have made certain demands.

ALAN: We exposed them to our friends. They saw different standards and interests and commitments to social issues which were important to us. There was also a lot of withhold-ing of respect for the values we didn't have. They knew it. They could feel it.

ESTHER: We did have standards. We did have goals for them. But I always very much rejected the idea of achievement per se. I always insisted as a person and as an educator that test scores and that kind of thing were of no concern. I always rejected conventional standards and said you have to make your own standards.

ALAN: Now, I expected high grades and got them. I think grades are an important benchmark to progress in this society, and if you don't pay attention to it, it's going to set you back and keep things from being available to you.

It took a long time for Abby to accept certain disciplines.

She wanted to be a creative person, a writer, but she was so ill prepared. Now she's writing for a newspaper, and she is learning as she's doing it.

I think you have to know what the rules are if you want to keep the game available to you. You can disadvantage yourself permanently by having a transcript that's inadequate. I had a childhood where sports were a necessity in order to be respected. But my daughters didn't need respect through sports, and my standards were too high when it came to playing competitive sports. So I stopped trying to get them to play. But they learned to ski—we went skiing on weekends together. They swim, and now they're going back to tennis.

Nina's traveling through Europe now—really experiencing different places and people. She's now returned to the point where she's ready to go to graduate school, something I was pushing two years ago, but she wasn't ready then. First she worked in a museum, then she was teaching emotionally disturbed teenagers—which was a hairy experience. She's very dedicated and idealistic.

She has been a vegetarian since she was fifteen, much to my horror. I had great difficulty in accepting this. Now I don't feel that it will set her back romantically and socially anymore. I tried to get them interested in classical music for the longest time. The standing joke is that they dreaded coming down Sunday mornings and hearing choral music. It wasn't until about four years ago that Nina came back to it on her own. She has a good collection and she loves it. Abby's beginning to listen to it also.

They both love to dance—to rock, to reggae. Nina gets great joy out of going to a discoteque with friends. I had great difficulty in understanding that, but then I saw it gave her great satisfaction, and she does it very well. So I learned to tolerate it. But I was just so surprised that this should be a part of her life, that a daughter of mine would be out at a bar dancing till all hours.

ESTHER: Abby was the odd one in the family. She was very different from Nina, and we had to learn to respect and accept that part of her that was so unique. We tried to give her confidence, and we learned to appreciate contemporary things from her.

She went to public school until 7th grade so she was more in touch with the neighborhood and the popular culture. She also worked as a waitress one summer in a fast food place in the resort town where we spent summers.

ALAN: That was her rebellion. It was not really how we wanted her to spend a summer.

ESTHER: She ran around with local kids that summer. They were bums. They would stay out late drinking. She was riding around in trucks at two in the morning. She rode on the back of motorcycles. These were guys who hunted. They were part of the American culture. We were awed by it. And here was Abby who was able to be comfortable with it. At the time, there were bad screaming scenes, but in retrospect I'm respectful of this ability of hers.

ALAN: She was careful who she brought around. They were redeemable in our minds.

ESTHER: She took a half year off from college to have a non academic existence for the first time since she was five. She worked ringing doorbells collecting funds for a consumer advocacy group. I would never be able to do that.

ALAN: That was sort of scary. She would go into these neighborhoods in the evening, then having to sell herself and sell this cause. We were astounded that she could do it. But of course, now it's more acceptable to drop out of college than it was.

ESTHER: She also went through a period of shoplifting with friends of hers in the city. That I didn't know about at the time. I found out about it when she told me. That was the most secretive she ever was. She also told me that she and her sister were experimenting with smoking the various herbs I had in the kitchen.

ALAN: Sometimes there were accusations of favoritism toward

Nina, who had recognition in and outside the home. But Abby is open—she's an open person. It's so wonderful.

ESTHER: We're the scared ones. We stay with people we feel comfortable with. And also in a snobbish way—you know—feeling a little superior to most of them out there. And it's Abby who can reach out and establish common grounds.

ALAN: Abby has expressed curiosity about homesexuality to us.

ESTHER: Yes, I have been nervous about that. Young women now are exploring the extents of feminism and the rejection of men. She has friends who are experimenting with it, and I'm very nervous about it. It would be a very overwhelming thing to me. But the overall blanket is the example of our love for each other and our marriage and our life.

I was shocked when, in emerging from late adolescence, they used to say, "I don't know if I'll ever get married." Nothing could hit me harder in the heart than to hear that. But then they explained that they could never make a marriage as good as ours—or find someone as wonderful as their Dad.

Now, in their twenties, I marvel at how much they've adopted our goals. Their friends are amazed at how involved they are with us. They think we're great and want to be like us!

ELIZABETH

"I was trying to communicate with my daughter, to recapture an intimacy that needed its own evolution."

Elizabeth has led a difficult but rich and varied life. The first child of a young and inexperienced mother, she was sent to live with her grandparents. Her grandmother, whom she adored, was totally disabled by a stroke when Elizabeth was seven, so in essence, she raised herself. Her ambition was always to be an actress, and she succeeded in the fiercely competitive New York theatre.

She married a handsome fellow actor, had three children and was deserted by him when her oldest child was ten. Years of struggle and privation followed until she met Mark; a dashing, charismatic man and a brilliant psychotherapist. Living with Mark inspired her to become a therapist herself. Mark had three boys of his own and Elizabeth found herself coping with six teenagers, a new and demanding career, and an intensely romantic personal relationship.

She has survived it all with strength and grace. She now has her own business, plays tennis and the piano daily, and is a gourmet cook. Yet even this model of competence and self-reliance had problems with her children. In this interview she speaks of Susanna, her only daughter, now twenty, an aspiring young actress, a delightful and exuberant young woman.

When Susanna became a pre-adolescent my feeling was one of bewilderment—really bewilderment because I felt that I was doing all the right things. I felt I was a good mother; loving, caring, supportive. I never beat my kids—I always had time for them. I couldn't understand why she was becoming alienated from me. I was terribly frightened and worried. Now I'm much more knowledgeable about the chaos that kids go through. I don't take it quite so personally because I know it's a transitory stage. I know now it's a process of kids finding their own identity, that they have to be confronting and they have to rebel.

Most kids do rebel. My kids did in varying degrees. Susanna and I didn't have problems that you ordinarily associate with parents and teenagers. For instance, there were no problems over sex, or drugs, smoking, or drinking or curfews. There were no wild parties. I liked her friends. I didn't have problems with authority. I wasn't a terribly authoritative mother, but she didn't really challenge me.

The problem was basically having a step-father that Susanna didn't like, and that created a great deal of tension that she took out on me. What I saw happening was that she closed me off. She grew away from me. She had a lot of substitute mother figures.

It made me feel terrible. I couldn't understand why she was turning away from me. She had a music teacher she adored. She adored all her father's girl friends and also my friend Sandy and her new baby. One time I called her into my room when she was spending all this time with Sandy, and I said, "I miss you, and I really feel badly because I don't see you very much, and we don't have much time together." And she said to me, "I really enjoy spending time with Sandy and the baby. Why do you want me to feel bad for doing something I enjoy?"

But I felt that she didn't enjoy spending time with me. For whatever reasons, for whatever her own needs were. Maybe she retaliated because she thought I was spending too much time with Mark. And I did spend a lot of time with Mark. And I also spent a lot of time at my job as a therapist because I was determined to make my own living, to provide for my kids when their own father wouldn't provide for them. And then she wanted to leave and stay with her grandmother in Indiana. She was a freshman in high school at the time. Her grandmother's a very maternal woman. I could see why she wanted to spend time with her. Also, she had friends and relatives there, and she would be the apple of her grandmother's eye instead of having to share with two brothers and three step-brothers. At first she wanted to stay one semester so I felt that wasn't so bad. Then in mid-year she wrote and said she wanted to stay the rest of the year. And she did.

When she came back to live with us, it was terrible. She was so combative, so confronting with Mark, so snippety. Susanna's a feisty, lively, young lady, very dramatic. She created a lot of turmoil. Finally, she announced that she was going to live in another town where we had once lived and would stay with her best friend and her family. Since I had always been so independent as a child, I have let all my children make some pretty independent decisions. I didn't tell her she couldn't move out just as I didn't forbid her to go live with her grandmother. Maybe, if I had to do it all over again, I would try to interfere a little more and be more demanding along those lines. I don't know. I do know that all my children are extremely independent people.

After she moved out this last time, we started to have a very good relationship. I felt that was so because she was maturing; the separation gave her a better sense of perspective. I also felt that we got on very well because I never tried to make her feel guilty for leaving. I felt sometimes like doing that, but I didn't. I kept in touch with her a lot, wrote her letters, called her on the phone, invited her out and was always interested in what she was doing.

After high school, we became even closer. During the rough years, she was very closed to me. I have tried to be as honest and open with my kids as I could, and so I felt very left out. Also, I knew that she talked openly to other women and friends. But once she graduated, she really began to talk to me. I think that one of the reasons for this was that she was having a lot of anxiety. She was seeing a shrink and having to deal with lots of repressed anger against her father. I've had my own share of anxiety attacks, and I know what they're like, so I felt I could be helpful and supportive. She would call me a lot, many times late at night when she'd be feeling awful. I never cut her off. I shared my own experiences with her, and that was the gate back to the kind of closeness I wanted.

One time I expressed to her some of my feeling of jealousy over her "courtship" of her father. (Since he had deserted my children years ago, when they finally started seeing him again, they were all very anxious to please him and gave him lots of attention.) She wisely said, "Mom, I don't have to run after you because you're always there for me." And those words meant a great deal to me.

Another thing that I used to do, looking back, was that when sometimes my kids would argue with me, I would get upset or bothered, and there'd be some kind of confrontation, and I would stutter and stammer like an idiot. I would get so emotionally involved that I couldn't be clear about what I meant what I thought and felt. It always felt like an unfinished situation to me, and I wanted them to know what I thought and felt. So I got into the habit of sitting down and writing a letter to them after it was all over. And I wrote a lot of those. Susanna later told me that she saved most of my letters because she always felt I gave such good advice. It was also a way to make things clear to myself.

Writing my thoughts down also meant that they could read them when they wanted to. They could meditate on them and both accept and reject certain things. And you don't have to rely on timing. They can read it when they're in the mood to do so.

Timing is important. Susanna and I would get messed up on our timing. When I was working as a therapist, I didn't have too much time. She always wanted me to come up and say goodnight to her when I was in the middle of leading a group. Maybe this was a ploy, maybe she wanted me to make a choice. For I was very busy with my groups, and I was busy with Mark. Now I realize there was a lot of jealousy. I was aware that she needed me. I'd make a plan to stay home on a certain night so we'd have time together. And then she'd say, "Oh, I forgot, I have plans tonight," and off she'd go.

Now it seems funny to me, but then it seemed very serious. I was trying to communicate with my daughter, to recapture an intimacy that needed its own evolution.

I wanted closeness with my children, but I believe in letting kids find their own way, and so, for whatever reason, Susanna needed adult substitutes—people to talk to. She felt a need and took care of it in a mature way. She really wasn't trying to hurt me. But if I had it to do all over again, I would try to be more aware of the turmoil. I would have made more time for my kids at the expense of making money.

In the area of sexuality, incidentally, I may have been more permissive than many mothers. I don't believe in one standard for sons and another one for daughters. I did not try to impose any of my own standards on her because I feel very strongly that one has to discover one's own sexual identity, and that might mean many things, including a certain amount of experimentation. I do feel that sex should be fun, loving, and guilt free; that one shouldn't take oneself too seriously, and that one should derive both humor and passion from one's sexual life. I hope that she has absorbed this; I think that she has, and she is very frank and open with me about this part of her life, also.

After their father left, I had such a terrible time trying to support us that I was determined never to put myself in that position again. I would still have worked, but I would have tried not to be so obsessive about it and would have made more time for them.

I also feel I was unaware—I shut my eyes—of how jealous the kids were of Mark and our relationship. He was a new person in the household taking up my time. I openly adored him, and I thought my children would want to share in this—

and they didn't. I should have spent more time being adoring with them. My kids wanted me to make a choice, to reassure them that they were my primary interest, and I don't feel that I did as good a job of that as I wanted to. But I also felt it was important for them to know that my husband was my primary interest as my mate, and they were my primary interest as my children. You would die for your children, but when you want to go out at night you go out with your husband. I wanted to be clear to them. I felt it was important to delineate those roles.

I have a very strong sense of values which I try to pass on to my kids. I'm full of silly old maxims and proverbs that I got from my grandmother. And I can see they've ingested a lot of them. Without realizing what I was doing, I passed on a lot of my values to my kids. They've adopted them for their own use. I have strong ideas of who I am and what I want, and that's helpful for kids because there's not ambivalence. I was very independent as a child, and I wanted my kids to do everything for themselves they could possibly do. There were two things I tried to stress to them. One is to be honest. The other is to work very hard at things that you love, and enjoy the work and not the results. I always told my kids it made no difference what kind of marks they got as long as they worked hard at what they were doing. I wanted them to enjoy the process. I learned as an actress that the process is what's exciting. And I look at my kids now, and I'm happy with their interest in a lot of things, their enthusiasm for working, their projects, their energy, their creativity. I wanted them to do things that they love because what they love will give them discipline for the process.

I felt that I did have a role model in my grandmother, and now I feel that Susanna looks to me as a role model more and more. In some ways she was competitive with me, but I can see me in her and her in me. She is very much her own person, but I feel that she knows very strongly that I am always there for her, and I feel or hope that this gives her a good sense of security and love.

ANITA

"But when Angela was graduating from high school and she came home and told me she was going to the senior banquet with this black boy, I was shocked!"

Among the immediate crises Anita had to deal with in rearing her children was that posed by her daughter's dating a boy of a different race—not an easy thing for a parent to deal with particularly when one comes from a working-class background. On a long-term basis there were also the problems of poverty and the alcoholism of her husband, Joe.

Joe's drinking meant that he was constantly losing a series of odd jobs, that income could never be relied upon, that his moods and temper were unpredictable, and that he was not able to set the tone for childrearing. This task was therefore undertaken by Anita, a handsome, competent woman who describes herself as the "domineering" force in her four children's upbringing. Her philosophy of child-raising was a combination of strict, old-fashioned values, personal honesty and a willingness to learn and change.

Today the children are grown, but all live within miles of Anita and Joe (who has given up drinking). Angela is a career woman involved in real estate and banking. Katie teaches elementary school and has just had her first child—Anita's first grandchild! Joe Jr. (Joey) has a landscaping business and Danielle is working, writing, and saving money for college. Their personal life styles and mores differ from their parents, but the family is still close and loving and in constant contact.

I was honest with them in every sense like even them knowing what we could afford and couldn't afford or how little we did have. They knew our circumstances at all times. I can't hide my feelings—I give myself away. I show my emotions very easily. I never hid anything—if something had to be said I said it. I didn't let things wait or build up. I didn't say. "Wait till your father gets home." As a result of all this they themselves are good in money situations and are aware of right and wrong.

I never worked until Danielle was in 5th grade and even then only part time, maybe two or three days a week. I was strictly family. I'm definitely a home person. When the kids were teenagers I worked days, but they were in school. And if they had a game or the girls were cheerleading or if Joey had a wrestling match, I left work early and I went home.

We did a lot of things together at home. We never had any income to go anywhere. We did take the kids to the world's fair. We ate dinner together every night—that was a must.

The kids started out in Catholic school but went to a public high school when we moved to the country. We went to church every Sunday. They all received their confirmations.

They helped out around the house. They had definite things they had to do. Even though I was home all the time I still insisted that everything had its place, so the house was constantly picked up and neat. They never had allowances. Money was very tight because we had a very, very low income from Joe. So whatever they needed they got, or whatever I could afford. They hardly went to movies—any function they went to was through school. And it wasn't until they were well into their teens—sixteen or seventeen—that they were allowed to go out. Not even on weekends until they were seventeen or so. Then they had a curfew. They had to be in or call. I had to know all the time where they were going and how they were coming home; whether it meant my taking them and going to pick them up at one o'clock in the morning when the party was over. Some of the kids parents were very lax about how their kids got around, and I couldn't stand that.

We lived seven miles out of the village, and I made constant trips—football, basketball, girl's things. Some days I made seven trips or more.

I told them when I didn't like their friends and what my reasons were. Sometimes I was wrong. I had always believed that I was not a prejudiced person especially since I have an uncle who's black. He's a light skinned Negro. and we always loved him. I accepted him so easily I felt I could accept any black person. We never, *never* in our home used the word nigger or anything like that. We had respect for everyone.

But when Angela was graduating from high school and she came home and told me she was going to the senior banquet with this black boy, I was shocked! Joe said, "No way." and Angela said, yes, she was going, that we had brought her up to respect all the kids in her class and she was going. We thought we were not a prejudiced family, and here we were saying no. I said, "Wait, maybe somebody else will ask you." And she said no, she wasn't going to wait. She had accepted. and there was no way she wasn't going to go.

Every day her father would come home and there'd be a fight and there'd be an argument and every day she would cry and say she wasn't going to tell him no, and that she was definitely going. And finally, one night after they went to bed, Joe and I were talking and I said, "She's right. All these years I thought I wasn't prejudiced. We brought them up to respect everybody no matter who they were or what they were, and now we're doing something we shouldn't be doing. We should tell her she should go." Joe wouldn't accept this at first, but I tried to make him understand. Because I felt something in me saying, "What are you doing?" All these years I thought I wasn't prejudiced, and here all of a sudden because it's my daughter it's become an issue.

I said, "Joe, it's not fair. She's right. We can't forbid it. She has to go with him." And he came to the house dressed beautifully and brought her a beautiful corsage.

I felt this experience was a growing thing for me. It made me look into myself. Later on, when my son Joey went to live with his girlfriend, I couldn't be critical of that. I had to respect his decision. I knew he wouldn't live with just anybody, and I respect him for this. And she's a very lovely girl. My daughter, Danielle, smokes, and I hate it. She knows I hate it. She knows my feelings. But I let her do it. You can't own them. You can love them and care for them, but you can't own them.

Manners!! Oh yeah. They go out the door today and I still say, from force of habit, "Mind your manners." Definitely manners. There's no two ways about it. They didn't curse at home. When Joey was about thirteen he came home and used the word "frigging." And I said "Forget it—there's no way. You can use that on the football field but not in front of your sisters or where any girls are." I myself curse. If anyone does use foul language in the house it's me. Joe doesn't use it. But I wouldn't allow the kids to curse.

I didn't discuss sex with the kids because they didn't ask. It never came up. But if they had asked me, I would have answered. Anything they have ever asked me I've answered. They have a great wariness for alcoholic excess because their father is an alcoholic. I'm sure they've tried marijuana and gotten drunk, but they don't overdo it.

Angela was valedictorian of her high school, Katie was always a 4.0 (A) student. Danielle is a brain and writes beautiful poetry. Joey was a mediocre student. I only pushed them according to their abilities. Once Danielle was making up her Christmas list, and she asked me what I wanted for Christmas, and I said "All I want is good kids." And they still remember that.

It sounds like everything was glory road but it wasn't. It was hard because of Joe's drinking and no money. But the kids weren't scarred; it made them self sufficient and strong. I think today I have the best relationship in the world with my kids. I learned from them. I have a friendship with them above just being their mother. Apart from loving them I like them. They're not carbon copies of me, but they're good people.

BILL

"I had my own problems to contend with . . . but I was deter-mined not to have a neurotic family situation."

Bill is a commerical artist, divorced, father of three, Ruth twenty-one, Louisa nineteen, and Doug seventeen. Like many parents he consciously strove to overcome his own unhappy child-hood, but unlike many parents he considers his attempt successful.

His dealings with his middle daughter Louisa, are less smooth than with his other two children. But Bill, though he's presently disturbed by his daughter's choice of a partner, remains objective and non-controlling. He admits this is difficult but still thinks it's the best thing to do.

My own childhood was really screwed up. I had an alcoholic father who left when I was five and a mother who was living in a fantasy world. She was literally a stage mother. I was a model and I was in films and I hated it. I felt like I was being used. Finally I had a nervous breakdown when I was eleven, and I couldn't work anymore. I was sent away to my father's sister's farm in Vermont for a year, and that was fabulous.

When I got married and decided to have children there was no question in my mind that they weren't going to go through the same routine. I never pushed them. I was not obedience minded, and I certainly wasn't perfect. I had my own prob-lems to contend with, but I realized the buck stopped with me. I was determined not to have a neurotic family situation. And I have succeeded to a large extent. There were no rules and regulations that were rigid. There was no need for that. They learned good behavior by example, not by force.

I remember once, years ago, I was very impressed by a man in Maine who had these two nice children. Some tourist asked the father—who was a native of Maine—"Your children are so nice, they're so well adjusted, they're so friendly. What do you attribute this to?" He said, "You gotta show em." Terrific. That's what I tried to do. The basic approach I've had is to remember not to lash out, or say that this is the way you should do it unless I did it that way myself. Only if I really felt it was a life threatening situation would I forbid it. Otherwise they could do what they wanted. I followed my instincts and still do. I've been as liberal and honest as I could with them.

I was very lucky that I was able to stop drinking. I had to conquer that and with the help of a lot of people I was able to do it. I learned a whole value system from A.A. and my life is much better. I'm so thankful for that. The children were a big factor in making me stop. They know I go to A.A. and they come to meetings sometimes. I never stopped them from drinking, but they knew all about me. I spoke to them personally about it, and they heard me speak at A.A. many times. But it would be crazy not to let them drink. Both Ruth and Louisa have experimented with grass and booze, but they don't do it to excess.

I haven't had any major problems, but the different stages of development in children present specific challenges. Pre-puberty is different than after puberty. I tried to take that into account, but the teenage years are when the real problems start. I have one daughter who tends to be somewhat self destructive, my middle daughter Louisa, the artist.

When my wife and I separated, the child who really felt it the most was Louisa. She was about thirteen. I saw her as much as possible, at least every weekend, but it was tough. Everybody was freaked out. I'd wake up in the middle of the night and think of the kids, and it would really hurt. Both my wife and I tried to be as mature as possible and not make the children victims.

Louisa also had a problem with a sibling rivalry situation with her sister Ruth who's now a senior at Yale and who's always done well—has been a high achiever. So I've always tried to encourage Louisa in her art; after all, I'm an artist. She has a tremendous amount of pizazz; she has everything going for her, and I tell her so.

I do have a good relationship with her except she's living with this guy. I called her a couple of months ago and this fellow answered and I said, "Excuse me, is Louisa there?" And he said, "Who's this?" and I said, "I'm Louisa's father, my name is Bill Kincaid, how are you? What's your name?" And he wouldn't answer me, and he wouldn't relate to me whatsoever. That really burned me up. First of all, he's not a teenager. I can understand a certain amount of teenage reticence, not being completely open with adults, a certain shyness. But this guy's twenty-seven years old, he's been married, he's divorced. I don't think I presented a threat to him, but obviously he's threatened by me in some way. I feel as though he should be able to communicate at least on a civil level. That's all I ask.

So I discussed this with Louisa one evening when she came over and I said, "I know you think I'm an Archie Bunker type because your boyfriend's Puerto Rican. I don't care what he is. That isn't the point. The point is, what kind of person is he? I have certain ideas about seeing you do as well as you can. I want you to find somebody who's a good partner, where the partnership's mutually beneficial."

I don't think he is a good partner for Louisa, that's my opinion, but obviously he's fulfilling a need that she has. And I don't want to pry. The tough thing is letting it go—but I'm doing it. I have to try to be as objective as I can and not try to control the situation which is sometimes very difficult.

On the other hand, my son Doug and I communicate very well. We play tennis together, we hang out together, we kid around a lot. He's a very earnest guy, and he's very honest and sincere. Once in a while we get into a little tiff but that's normal. Basically we have an excellent relationship. And I feel that with all of my children, I've done the best job that I could.

JUDY

"It seemed like she wanted me to be setting limits."

Judy is young, vibrant, athletic, intelligent, and teaches elementary school in a medium size western city. She began her parenting permissively but felt a need for more order and continuity after she split up with her husband. She was also able to intuit the different needs of her children. She allowed Justin to go live with his "loose" father, but she insisted that Catherine stay with her.

As Catherine grew into adolescence Judy felt the need to impose more restraints and did so, not to be arbitrary, but because certain aspects of Catherine's behavior made her uncomfortable. Judy grew into her responsibility as a mother as her children grew. Justin and Catherine are now independent and interesting adults who take responsibility for their own lives maintaining affectionate ties to their mother. Judy says of her daughter Catherine, "our relationship just gets better and better."

After Sam and I split up I was seeing a psychiatrist. He recommended a book by Dreikurs called *Children the Challenge*. This book was the best thing I have ever, ever, ever read. It made perfect sense. I wanted to end the general atmosphere of turmoil and to start being consistent, reasonable, and simple in dealing with the kids. This was all covered in the book so I was real happy to try that stuff out.

But Justin sort of flipped out when I did it. He was probably too old (fourteen) to start a different routine. The idea of logical consequences is central to Dreikurs. For example, the business of being home for dinner at a certain time. If Justin didn't come home to dinner he didn't get any dinner because it would be over when he got home. I think it was absolutely the right way to do it. But Justin was a big kid, and I'm standing in the doorway saying, "I'm sorry, the kitchen's closed. You're not going to have anything. I'll look forward to seeing you tomorrow. Hope you can make it." He was in a rage, and big enough to push me down. We had a few real strong confrontations.

Justin knew that Sam was real loose and that Sam was hardly ever home and was easy to work around. Plus my household was a household of women. It was Catherine and me and a female roomate and Justin—and he didn't like it. He wanted to be left alone and do what he wanted to do and not be hassled by somebody who's now trying to be an effective parent. So he moved in with Sam when he was fifteen. I didn't feel like I could say no. I remember being depressed about it, but I was gearing up to move to the west coast, and I knew he didn't want to come so it made it easier for me to move. So it was pretty untraumatic.

And it worked fine for Justin. When he visits here, about once a year, it's wonderful. Everybody is crazy about him—all ages, all types of people. He makes everybody feel good. He wins people over in the nicest way.

On the other hand, when Catherine got to be about fourteen she said she also wanted to move back to Chicago and live with Sam. I told her she couldn't do it, that it was against all my principles. I felt I didn't want to handle our difficulties in that way. And we were having difficulties. She was staying out late, she was being irresponsible, she'd climb out of her bedroom window in the middle of the night and run off to Charlie's Pool Hall. She was sleeping with some guy then. I didn't know about that till later. It was real hard on her—he was real shitty to her. Then somebody told me about it—the mother of a friend—who assumed that I knew. I confronted Catherine and I said something like, "I have the feeling that you didn't tell me these things because you thought I would disapprove of you for doing them. But I just want you to know that I would never disapprove of you." She didn't start to cry or anything, but her face just fell apart, and she looked enormously relieved.

She now tells me a whole lot. We talk about our sex lives pretty openly. I try to do this because I want to make sure she's getting everything she can. I mean that if she's sleeping with somebody she's doing it because she wants to, and it's real good for her not just because some guy wants her to.

I had boyfriends all along, usually one boyfriend at a time, but various men stayed with me. I never tried to shoo them out in the morning before the kids got up—or cared if the kids saw us lying in bed together. I didn't want to try to pretend that my life was something it wasn't. I didn't talk explicitly about my sexual feelings, but I guess by my behavior I made it pretty clear that sex was an important part of my life.

We talked about birth control, but Catherine didn't get a diaphragm until she was a junior in high school and she was visiting her father. She went and got it herself which I thought was really gutsy. And she told her father about it because she wanted him to pay the doctor bill.

Another problem I can remember with Catherine. She has this really beautiful body and she used to dress, to my way of thinking, outrageously, very sexually flamboyantly, to go to school. For a long time I felt this was none of my business, that she had the right to dress any way she wanted, but then I decided I couldn't stand it, that I didn't want her going out of the house looking like a whore, it was making me feel too uncomfortable. I'd always tried to be real fair, really democratic, and not just arbitrary. So when I started saying, "Change your dress, or "Button your shirt up," she was real powerful in protesting. She knew all the things that would get me like, "That's not fair. You have no right to tell me that. You've never done this before, why are you telling me this now?" I said, "I'm not going to stand by while you go down the drain, that would be abdicating my responsibility as your mother." Eventually it passed, for whatever reason, she got into levis and plaid shirts like the rest of us.

We had a big fight about food too. I found out she was taking her lunch money and buying cokes and chocolate bars—that's all she was eating. I wouldn't give her any more money for lunch. She was very indignant, but I said, "You know as much about nutrition as I do, but you choose to act like an asshole, and I'm not going to let you do that. I'm going to do what I can to stop you. My job is to get you safely grown up and then when you're on your own you can eat chocolate bars and shakes." And of course, she doesn't.

We would have these fights that just decked me, real powerful verbal matches. She was a real hard match for me. But I would just stick to my guns, and at the end of them she would always look relieved. That's what she wanted. It seemed like she wanted me to be setting limits.

We fought about her walking alone at night by herself. She was real flippant about that. I told her about being raped; the incidence of rape in our city is incredible. I told her everything I could to appeal to her reasonably. Then I said, "If you can't do it for yourself, you can do it for me. What kind of shape do you think I'd be in if you were raped?" And she was still very defiant, so I just wouldn't let her go.

Catherine had a need to explore, to find her own style, plus a lot of peer pressure. Now, at twenty, she has a super ego that's probably going to kill her; like me and Sam. She now wants to be civilized and cultured and intellectual like her grandparents. Her grades are much better in college than they ever were in high school. When I visited her last weekend, she was writing a paper. I went running, and she just sat down and did it. She's taking linguistics, real hard stuff. There was a time when she put down stuff like that. She plays raquetball and walks a whole lot. She's interested in museums and culture and wants to get out of Oregon even though she loves it because it's so beautiful. I hope she'll eventually come back and live near me. Our relationship just gets better and better.

JUSTINE

"I used to get him out of bed screaming, " 'Get down here! Your stuff's all over.' That wasn't too effective."

Justine's specific problem with Brad—getting him to do household chores—while familiar to most parents, was compounded by the fact that she is crippled by polio and can navigate only with a wheel chair or a leg brace and crutches.

Other concerns of hers have had to do with the values Brad would incorporate from the highly conservative community she and her husband Martin moved to when Brad started high school. Both Justine and her husband, Martin, are intellectual, highly educated professionals who had lived in a lower class neighborhood in a medium sized city. Justine is a psychologist and the president of a nationally known foundation for a crippling illness and Martin a former college professor who is now a lawyer for Legal Aid.

Justine and her husband are urbane, cultured, idealistic and fiercely liberal and—were it not for their desire to see their son attend a supposedly superior school system—they would still be living in the inner city. But their move to a posh suburb inhabited by corporate executives has, to their dismay, resulted in their son's being influenced and affected by values they themselves do not share.

Still, it is the nuts-and-bolts of tasks and enforcement that threatened her relationship with her son, yet it was a problem she ultimately dealt with successfully.

The most serious problem I had with Brad was getting him to help me clean the house. Tasks have to be done and cause me a great deal of frustration since I can't move easily. Many times it was just a matter of force. I'd yell at him. He was obedient and didn't yell back at me. But in fact I didn't care what he said to me as long as he did what I said. He made no effort to make me think that he's doing it because he wants to. He wants the house to look nice, but he doesn't want to do the work.

Actually, once his girlfriend was coming to visit and he cleaned the house. He knows what to do. But no matter how many times I'd tell him, I'd come home from work and his jock bag is on the table, his shoes and sneakers are on the table, his jackets are thrown all over the place. Just this year he's finally starting to pick things up, but he's still a little careless about monitoring things. He will leave his cereal bowl out, and not put it in the dishwasher.

I used to get him out of bed screaming, "Get down here! Your stuff's all over." That wasn't too effective. It got done, but he was mad and I was mad. So I finally said, "I can't stand this. It makes me furious. I know you don't care about it, but I do. I want you to do certain things. I need you to do certain things." And he said, "But I'm so busy. I have a lot to do." And I said, "I do too." So we made up a list. He has to vacuum and he does the laundry. He helps with the gardening under duress.

Picking up the house was definitely one of our worst problems because it was such a fight, such a conflict. There was a period of time when he was interested in sports solely. I wasn't sharing anything else with him. Brad and Martin have this whole thing with baseball. I don't get into it. I don't pretend to . . . though I try to understand what's going on, and I go to some of his sports events to watch him play. But at this point playing games with Martin was completely satisfying to Brad. Martin was his best friend, and Brad has been very spoiled by Martin. And I was left out of that team. The only relationship I had with them was fighting over the house-cleaning. Martin is so careless and unmindful about the house even when he's trying to be helpful that I have to yell at him also all the time. And I yell at Brad even more than Martin. There was almost nothing positive happening. The only thing that remained a positive aspect is that Brad continued to consider me his advisor if he had a problem with school or friendships.

Brad's relationship to me is largely based on counseling him on how to handle himself. He's a timid, fearful person, afraid of any new situation. I talk to him about his shyness, and I give him ideas as to how to talk to people, specific suggestions. I tell him how to try to make eye contact with people, how to say hello in a loud voice, how not to mumble. I practice with him. I gave him a book on manners, on how to shake hands, how to introduce friends to people. He read it and apparently has been able to act on it. Just this year he has developed some very intense friendships, and he's had a girlfriend since June.

He asked me once before he went to high school what a guidance counselor was. So I was telling him, and he said, "Oh you mean they provide you with counselors in school like I've always had personally with you?" Now, he's beginning to make fun of me. He says, "Oh, you think you know everything." And I'm glad. I don't want him to be a totally dependent kid.

But in any case, there was a time when it was purely negative. He was totally involved with Martin and sports and there was very little that we did that was fun together. I got a cleaning service to come in to do the heavy cleaning, and that made a big difference. We remodeled the attic for his room, and since I don't have to look at his room, I don't enforce him about picking it up. When he slept downstairs, I would insist that he clean his room because I could see it. But once he moved upstairs, I don't go up there. But until I did these things it used to be horrible. I would scream and yell. I tried to keep it focused on that particular area of anger and not let it generalize. Now he does the minimum. He does the laundry very reliably and well. He takes everything of his and leaves it on the stairs, but as long as it's out of my sight I don't care.

He's fabulously groomed and amazingly efficient. He gets up at six, takes a shower, gets himself done up. He's very quiet, he's very mindful of my needs, he doesn't have the radio on, keeps the lights down and goes off. He's always been very independent in taking care of himself; he has to be.

He worked on and off as a paper boy, but he doesn't like to work. He works now for the guy next door doing lawn maintenance. He has to rake and mow around here too. We give him money when he needs it. I used to give him an allowance, but he doesn't need all that much money. I buy his clothes, and I'll pay for his college. I've saved a lot of money for that. He doesn't abuse money, and I tell him that I won't be giving him money forever. I expect him to do well in school. That's his job. That, and helping me around the house.

He does well in school work without any effort and without any apparent anxiety. He's very well organized, he does his home work at a scheduled time. He comes home, sits down and does it. I've never had anything to do with his schoolwork. We've never had to enforce homework rules. That seems to have been internalized. It came easily to him and he likes to get good grades. He's now torn between socializing quite a lot, listening to his music, and his homework. He's achievement oriented so this is causing him a little concern.

I'm disappointed that he doesn't enjoy reading. We did a lot of reading to him, and Martin and I spend a lot of time reading, but Brad doesn't read. He read when he was younger, but as he got to be a teenager the social aspect became very important. He's very other directed right now. He's different from me. He's an individual with characteristics that I've had to adjust to. I never assumed I could totally mold him—not completely anyway. There are a lot of characteristics of mine I wouldn't want him to have. I wouldn't want him to have a lot of anxiety. I've tried to minimize that. I gave him a lot of attention and a lot of skills. He's well organized, he can concentrate, he can rationalize. He can think, and he's calm about it. I don't know where he gets his mathematical ability, but in thinking about it I wonder if it's not because he doesn't have a lot of anxiety.

We live in a highly conforming area, and the "heads"—the potsmokers—are a very small minority in his high school. Brad does not admire them at all. He looks down on them. He thinks there's something wrong with them, and they are not interesting to him. He only drinks and smokes (pot) in social situations because he supposed to. That's not a problem for me. I'm much more worried about whether or not he cleans the house than whether he smokes dope. . . . He's not particularly interested in having some dope with us. But he does smoke with his friends.

He's very oriented towards his peers; he's very shy so he needs a long period of time to get adjusted to people. It's important to him to be accepted as an athlete and a good student. He's a good athlete but not a great one. He's not big and he's worried about that. He says, "What am I going to do? I can't stand it. My legs are so skinny and I'm so small." And I say, "Look, just accept it. If you're going to be 5'7", you're going to be 5'7". Now work on the rest of yourself. . . . 5'7" is already acceptable, and there's nothing we can do about it, and there's nothing you can do." I really don't spend too much time sympathizing. I say, "I'm sorry you suffer over it, but you have to try to think more clearly about it. You're making too much of an issue about it. You have friends, you have a girlfriend, you're popular. It's not like you're being shunned." He's so critical of himself, so self conscious.

I'm glad he has friends. His friends are very pleasant, very nice kids. They're not super-spectacular, fantastic, fascinating people by any means, but they're good friends to him, and he's comfortable with them, and that's where he is right now. I'm glad he has his girlfriend. They have a close relationship.

He talks to her for hours on the phone every night. She's his confidant. . . . Gina's mother likes him. She's real pleased with him as her daughter's boyfriend. She likes him to visit and likes to take him places. I'm glad he's growing close to someone outside the family. I think it will help him to develop maturity.

He has a driver's license now, so he can go visit his friends. When he first started to drive I was a wreck. I had a cold for three weeks. I would say to him. "I'm a wreck. I have asthma. I feel like I can't breathe. My throat is closing up. All because you have gotten your driver's license. I can't stand it. How am I going to survive this period? I think you're going to get killed driving that car, and I'm hysterical." And he laughs and says, "I know how you feel, but I've got to be able to grow up. I have to be able to drive without you." So I said to him, "I want you to know if you're going to be out past midnight I'm going to be worried, and therefore I want you to tell me where you are." He thinks it's funny, but he does call. And if he's going to be a half hour late at suppertime, he'll call too.

I also notice that he has selected friends that he seems able to dominate. They are devoted to him, and sometimes when I hear him talking to them I can hear myself talking. He's taking on my point of view and is beginning to present himself as somewhat of a liberal to these kids. He's careful though, he doesn't want to be too way out. He used to be embarassed if I played rock music on the car radio when his friends were in the car.

He's trying to conform very carefully to what he sees around him because we are different from everybody else here, and he knows that. It makes him feel insecure that we don't have the same values and don't act the same way the other parents do. We don't have a big house, we don't have five couches and a family room with a color T.V. and it makes him feel different and insecure with his peers. I've been telling him that he's living a sheltered existence that is not very great. I'm sorry that we moved here other than the pleasantness of the surroundings for myself. It is a deprivation, and I didn't even realize it would be so. I didn't think it would be so narrow, so rigid. But Brad likes it here and wants to be accepted. I try to give him as much encouragement as I can to be an individual. But I have to let him go his own way.

Now, I think that we have a good relationship basically. We're very close. He talks to me about everything, his feelings, sex. I take time with him after school when he doesn't have sports. He is interested in homosexuality now. He's trying to understand it and is curious about it. He's very, very uncomfortable with some of my lesbian friends. He has prejudices against them, and that bothers me. I don't like that narrowness that he's showing, and I tell him so.

But mostly I'm interested in him being as psychologically healthy as possible. That's my main expectation of him. I won't be particularly disappointed if he doesn't achieve a certain kind of success or a certain kind of marriage, or certain kinds of friendship patterns. I don't have an investment in that. I just want him to be pleased with what he does. I don't want him to be neurotic and fucked up. As he slowly comes into himself, he'll have to make decisions on how he wants to live. We've given him a value structure as best we can, and it's up to him to take it.

JONAS

"My poor wife loved her daughter and she loved me too. I couldn't throw the kid out, or force the mother to choose between her child and me."

Jonas is an attractive, athletic professional man who appears carefree and very much in control of his life. He is not easily cowed professionally or socially but is definitely what psychologists term a "risk taker." Yet, according to him, he was nearly undone by the teenage daughter of his second wife.

He speaks openly but emotionally about his feelings and about how he was finally able to express himself in a "creative" way after countless attempts at compromise, and not come out a "loser."

When I met Cathy she had three children. The one that I had the absolute most difficulty with was her daughter. The two boys I got on fairly well with. The daughter was a great animal lover, and I had an allergy to cats. The daughter had a cat and five kittens and as soon as I moved in I was wheezing and getting asthmatic attacks. It was obvious the cats had to go or I had to go. So the cats went. This did not endear me to the daughter. In addition to that, Cathy was very lovey-dovey with me—she spent a great deal of time with me which bothered Melissa a lot. I know at one time Cathy came across a little diary of Melissa's—she was maybe twelve or thirteen—talking about how jealous she felt of me.

One of Cathy's great hopes was that we'd be one big, happy

family. Since her former husband was an alcoholic, I'd be a new role model—a decent person—and the kids at last, would have a family. She did her damndest to make us all like each other. She'd explain them to me, explain me to them. We'd have family dinners—attempts on her part and mine to be friendly.

But there wasn't much reciprocity on Melissa's part. She'd leave the house in a tremendous mess; socks, clothes, food, all over the place. I would get so annoyed I'd put stuff in boxes and leave it outside, or I'd throw her things out on the lawn. I didn't feel like being a maid to anyone.

All of these things were not viewed kindly. She'd say things like, "You're not my father. You can't tell me what to do." And sure enough I wasn't. But I did live in the house.

There was a build up of mutually antagonistic feelings and resentments and jealousies. And the more we would resent each other, the more Cathy tried to make us peaceful and loving and create a nice family scene. There were all these subtle things. We'd sit at the table, and there'd be an animated conversation with great smiles going on between Cathy and the kids. "Do you remember Aunt Tu Tu and Uncle Goo-Gaw and Freddie, and what we did when I was three years old?" Everything would focus on a time of life that I was never involved in, with great hilarity and smiles.

And then they would look around, like here's the present, and it was, "Pass the butter." and a steely look implying "What are you doing here, you drip?"

I heard the same stories over and over again. It was like people on a dope high, only it all focused on the past. I felt like an outsider for they treated me like an outsider, particularly Melissa. I wasn't as good as their father, I wasn't as smooth as their father, I didn't have the same tastes as their father. So I would try to do things differently than their father. He always broke his promises so I was very meticulous about keeping my word. And it didn't mean shit. Melissa just wanted me to make more promises.

I remember she wanted a bicycle for Christmas one year, and I got her a really nice one. What I got was a half smile and a perfunctory handshake, and then she proceeded to ooh and ah over a bar of soap from her father. She was also going out and complaining to people about the quality of life in our house, how hard it was to live with my "rules"; like clean up your dishes or pick up your clothes.

And Cathy and I started to have a lot of fights about it all. Our idyllic relationship turned into squabbling. Cathy would try to mediate, and we spent increasing time out of the house to avoid the whole situation. Our priorities were to enjoy each other and be good parents too. Cathy was on my side a lot which made Melissa even nastier.

Meanwhile, I was forming a good relationship with Cathy's son but Melissa started poisoning his head too. Then he started giving me flak. I wasn't even talked to; they ignored me except when they wanted to use my car. Here I was shelling out dough for someone who hated me. And again, my poor wife loved her daughter—and me too. I couldn't throw the kid out, or force the mother to choose between her child, and me.

Then Melissa went away one summer to camp, and it felt wonderful. But when she came back the well was poisoned again. She kept saying she wanted to go to boarding school, but she couldn't make up her mind.

One day I was driving around with Melissa in the car, she in her usual sullen state, when a light bulb went off in my head; it was truly a eureka phenomenon. I said to her, "Melissa I realize that you're not such a bad person and I'm not such a bad person but you make me feel like a piece of shit and I must make you feel that way too. And I think the person who's really the bad person in all of this is your mother. Because your mother wants us to like each other. And we're just ordinary people and somehow the chemistry's not right and we don't like each other that much. If we were just at a distance we wouldn't dislike each other, we'd just be neutral. But the fact that we always have to eat together and play together and be together is driving us crazy. And that's your mother's fault.

"I find it's impossible for me to live in the house with you. If you're not going off to school next year, I'll move out. You can live with your mother. I'll get a room in a house down the block. I can still date and visit your mother. I'll have a good time with her. That way you can have your mother, I can have your mother, and we won't be at each other's throats anymore."

She gave me one of her sullen looks and said, "I'll think about it and let you know." And within three days she came to me and said—"I've decided to go away to school." And I said, "O.K." with a great feeling of relief. So she went away to school. And ever since then when she comes back to visit, we've gotten on famously. We went from total hate, to her treating me cordially, and then to her actually liking and accepting me. I enjoy her now. We chat a bit. I even talk to her about things she doesn't talk to her mother about.

I think this has to do with me conceding the fact that I couldn't struggle with her anymore. She had won. I gave up. That puzzled her. I acknowledged her as a powerful adversary and that I couldn't compete with her anymore. I was willing to undergo a major life change to accomodate her. I was utterly serious in my offer.

I feel it was a creative way to try to do something different. The actuality was that she went away to school, and our life went on. If I'd moved down the block, it would have been equally successful. And today, four years later, she tells me she can't even remember what we used to fight about.

CLAUDIA

"Living with Zachary made me realize that when I have my own son . . . I'm sure I'm going to have sexual feelings."

Claudia is a fashion model and actress. Her lover, Simon, is a psychiatrist. Her "stepson" Zachary is a mature boy only 10 years her junior. So Claudia had to face the usual mundane problems of living with a teenager, moodiness, sloppiness, sensitivity, insecurities, plus an awareness of a mutual sexual attraction.

When I first met Zachary he was fifteen and I was twenty-five. I was ten years older than Zachary and ten years younger than Simon. My first summer with Simon, Zachary lived with us for two months. He came from Colorado to visit his dad for the summer. Instantly our rapport was established in that we were clearly the people who took care of things in the household. We took care of groceries and the dishes. Simon was the one who had the money and he wanted to swim and run—those were his main concerns—so the issues of what to bring to the beach, who would make the sandwiches, who would pack the ice chest, fell to Zachary and me. We were sort of conspirators in the sense of complaining to each other. At this point it was very lighthearted because I was in love. It was a kind of banter about how Simon was lazy; we catered to him—it was all done in the spirit of comraderie. Zachary and I were two kids in the sense that we got along well but in terms of who was really responsible, Simon was the kid.

What struck me about Zachary from the very beginning was how mature he was, how you could talk to him. I hadn't been around a fifteen year old boy since I'd been a fifteen year old girl. I was uncomfortable when Simon and Zachary used to fight. Simon was very critical of Zachary. He would say, "You have your head up in the clouds. You're a dreamer." Of course, Simon was talking about himself, but I didn't see it at this point. Zachary would be very embarassed to be criticized in front of me, and he would become very defensive. And the two of them would argue. But at that point Zachary couldn't be as obnoxious and manipulative as Simon so he would always lose and get angry and storm out of the house yelling, "I don't want to talk about it." I took Simon aside and said, "Don't be so attacking of Zachary. You're not going to get anywhere by criticizing him." It then became a family dispute, and I was the mother protecting the delicate sensibilities of the son, and Simon a typical bullying father.

Zachary was very polite to me. He liked me; he helped me. He didn't relate to me as a mother figure; he treated me as a friend. Zachary talked to me about his feelings. We had amazing conversations about the meaning of life. At age fifteen he had already read all the Carlos Castaneda books. He was a very conscious kid; he was not your typical teenager. He loved to cook so we split the cooking of the meals. He was not a saint. He could be quite moody and slept a lot. I would get up in the morning, Simon would already be at the beach and Zachary would sleep till two in the afternoon. That annoyed me, but I remember doing that too. So I just treated it as a mild inconvenience.

Our second summer together he was a little more grown up. He had grown several inches all around, and I remember I was trying to come to terms with whether I should be naked around Zachary. The first summer I wasn't. I was always very careful to be clothed. Simon used to invite him into the bedroom at night when the two of us were in bed, and I was a little uncomfortable because this wasn't a child—this was a fifteen year old boy. I wondered how he saw me. Did he see me as a woman in bed with his father? At that point I don't know what he thought about it.

The second summer, when he was sixteen the change was immediate. When he got off the plane he kissed me on the mouth, with a lot of knowledge about kissing girls. It was like he was really a young man—he was looking at me differently. He looked great. He had cut his hair, and he had a wonderful body. I suddenly saw that Zachary was somebody who had made love to women. I remember one night—it wasn't August yet so Simon was only out on weekends so Zachary and I were alone during the week—anyway this night, we were lying in bed watching television like we had done many, many nights, and all of a sudden I became aware of this tension. I had the idea, what would it be like to sleep with Zachary? It was very appealing, and it was definitely a mutual fantasy, but of course I put it absolutely away in its place. It was not appropriate, to say the least.

But when Zachary was seventeen he came to live with us full time. Then the competition between Zachary and Simon really surfaced. Finally Zachary felt strong enough to stand up to Simon. I was the prize. If I could have run off with Zachary, it would have been the ultimate victory over his father—it's a classic Freudian situation. The relationship between Simon and me was deteriorating so all of the things Zachary and I complained together about during the summer were now serious problems; the fact that Simon was irresponsible, the fact that I acted like a drudge housewife, that I had rearranged my entire life to accomodate Simon. Zachary was terribly concerned about me and terribly considerate to the point where I was uncomfortable with it. The feeling I had was that he was saying, "If you went off with me, I wouldn't treat you like this."

So I spent a tremendous amount of time developing our relationship into a non-sexual friendship. We would have dinner out together, I would be sure to ask him about his life, girls at school, and all of that. Zachary was always in the living room because Simon was using his bedroom as an office. I would come home from working, and he would be there. It was like living in a studio apartment with somebody and he wasn't my lover, and he wasn't my son. I would come home from work and start making dinner, and he'd be sitting there. I always felt he wanted something from me. I told him he couldn't require so much of my attention. He felt very hurt, and I felt like I was being unfair.

Then Simon finally got an office space so Zachary had his own room back, but he would still come into the living room with me. He didn't like spending time alone. And now that the apartment no longer had to keep its best face up for patients, the mess from Zachary's bedroom was creeping into the rest of the house. I had to assume the role of saying to Zachary, "I think it's time for you to clean your room up." I was not well cast for the role, but I did it. He was eighteen years old now, and I felt he was being an irresponsible slob. He was hurt by this, but he would go into his room and clean it up.

I do regret letting him in on so much of what was bad in my relationship with Simon. I never gave him blow by blow descriptions of our fights and difficulties, but I should have shown more self control and maturity and kept that separate from my interaction with him. Zachary has a history of witnessing bad relationships and mine with his father was another one. Not that I wanted to idealize it but I shouldn't have burdened him with it. But frankly one of the things that kept me in that relationship was Zachary. I really felt so much love for him, and I felt so responsible. I helped him choose his college, I went to the interviews with him. I took him to buy his first suit. He was so excited, and I had a great time. The sales people were very confused about our relationship which we enjoyed immensely. Now he's in college, and he always calls me when he comes home. I haven't seen him for a year because he's in Paris studying art, but the connection is still there.

Living with Zachary made me realize that when I have my

own son, if he's an attractive young man, I'm sure I'm going to have sexual feelings. Not sexual in the sense that I'll be afraid to be alone in the house with him but an appreciation of this boy, or girl's sexuality. Those teenage years were so dreadful for me, for everybody. I'm so glad I had an opportunity to be really supportive.

PETER

"I always felt I had something to learn from David. Not specifically sexually, but I did feel I could grow by learning how it was to be gay."

Peter was thirty when he met Anne, a woman of forty with a sixteen year old son. Anne and her son David had lived happily together for years. Peter was the first man to enter her life since David's father left them. By Peter's own admission his nature and David's appeared diametrically opposed. David was a reserved, intellectual boy and gay. Peter was outgoing, ebullient, and straight. But Peter was determined to overcome the differences between them and, despite David's initial resistance and resentment, he succeeded.

When Anne and I first got together it was kind of on a fly by night, gypsy like level. Her son being a responsible young man, a Capricorn, and homosexual was, I felt, extremely disdainful of my flippant habits, my lustful and quasi-outrageous behavior toward his mother. One never knows where homosexuality comes from, but there was certainly a strong bond between him and his mother.

And there I was, appearing literally out of the night, his mother's suitor—this outrageous, footloose character—and, I suppose to his eyes, quite macho, though I tried not to push this. I felt a lot of judgmental attitudes on his part. I would get drunk and carry on. Anne and I had voluminous sex, and it was a small house. Either there was total silence or curious little judgmental statements about my habits, my noise, my mess, my this and that.

The reasons were obvious, but my reaction was to persist in relating directly on his level. I didn't try to figure out where it was coming from. Rather than get at some psychoanalytical roots I tended to specifically deal with the immediate situation. I refused to be at all furtive about my sexual connection with his mother. I was free about it. I tried not to rub it in his face, but there was no avoiding it. I couldn't hide the joy that I felt, and that was confusing to him.

Also, at that time, his own sexuality was a mystery and a source of a lot of problems for him. He was trying to resolve who and what he was. I never avoided his problems; I never avoided talking to him. Obviously, in the situation, he wasn't totally available to me, but I wouldn't be put off. I would express concern about him; I joked with him about his sexuality. I didn't allow any of it to become devious. I let it all be what it was.

I'd jab him once in a while about being gay, and it would get him to make a statement—sometimes observational, sometimes defensive. David's generally a circumspect and judgmental person but an intelligent person too. He had a lot of insight into what he was going through and into what was going on around him. He found the hetero—quote—macho way of relating completely disgusting (and I must confess, it *is* rather disgusting).

I was curious about him, not having had that much homosexual experience myself. I didn't abhor anything he was going through. I could also relate to him on the level that he was sixteen years old and going through all of the horrendous, embarrassing, problematic situations that I went through. I didn't find it so different from my adolescent experiences. I listened to him, and he began to speak more and more freely. He opened up more and began to realize that our problems were similar regardless of our sexual proclivities.

I always did show a lot of respect for him. His intelligence made me cautious about not bullshitting because he wouldn't accept this. I couldn't afford to be slipshod in my thinking or my comments. I paused and considered before I spoke. I didn't want to make him my enemy, and I didn't want him to think I was a fool. I had no preconceived reaction to homosexuality. He would do some flagrant things to test me. Like dancing around in front of me—being particularly flaming. His make up would be a little more outrageous than usual or his patchouli (perfume) a little heavier. And I got a kick out of it. Or he'd start describing some classical homosexual encounter, and I'd proceed to describe some equally ridiculous heterosexual encounter. And we'd both laugh.

We'd get to it a lot on a laughing level. I think that was very important—a sense of humor. It was like he was saying— "This is the way I live. What do you think?" And I'd say— "It's a gas, but it's a problem sometimes. I have problems too, and they're very similar." I could do this because I basically always knew he was a good person. I saw how he related to other people and to his mother, and that was enough for me. I also felt a genuine physical attraction for him, and I didn't have any inhibition or reticence about showing my affection physically. The acceptable heterosexual trip is that men are supposed to shake hands and go "Hey!" and slap each other on the shoulder. But from the very beginning I would hug him and kiss him. Maybe David found this surprising, but that's just the way I am. And I think he liked it.

I remember when the barriers finally came down. Anne had moved back into the city, and we were seeing each other only on weekends. It was a difficult time for me—I was feeling a lot of anxiety and loneliness. David was away at prep school so we saw each other only on his vacations in the city. One time he came in to visit, and we were standing in the kitchen of Anne's tiny apartment, and he started talking about a relationship he was having with this man—a very young man—even younger than himself. He was talking in a very real way about his concern and the fact that he was less committed to the relationship than his lover. He was worried because he didn't want to fuck this person up. It was an extremely adult conversation. Things were no longer just happening to him. Suddenly he was the active responsible party in the situation—showing concern for someone else. Also he was having strong feelings for another person and missing him. So it was like we were at last on the same level. David was experiencing a powerful sexual connection, and now he understood me better. That's what helped the most.

One major aspect of this whole evolution is that I always felt I had something to learn from David. Not specifically sexually, but I did feel I could grow from learning how it was to be gay. And I think he learned things from me—to be more accepting, for instance. And that people can be different in their habits but still have something very strong in common—a very important base. And now, after five years, our attachment to each other is so strong I cry when he leaves for college after our summers together.

JOANNE

"I made sure his life wasn't a bore."

Craig was born when Joanne was twenty. Ten months later she left her husband because of his "incesscant drinking" and his "smacking her around." Craig has not seen his father since.

She went home to live with her parents who took care of Craig while she went to beauty school. Craig's grandparents have been instrumental in his upbringing. Joanne's father always did things with the boy, fishing, boating, home projects.

Today Joanne owns her own business in a fashionable resort community, gardens, plays golf, has a busy social life. Craig is in his first year at college. He is a superb athlete, an outstanding student, socially outgoing and popular—a real leader—as independent and competent as Joanne herself.

Craig was never left alone. In the summer he went to day camp or my mother watched over him. On Saturdays when I worked he had to fend for himself, but my mother was around, and he had to check in and out and tell her where he was going. He would always leave me a note if he was going to be gone when I came home from work. I was always home for dinner, and I fed him breakfast every morning.

He always had a curfew. He was not allowed to go out on school nights except to certain school events and then only if his homework was done. Then he'd usually be home by nine or nine-thirty. On weekends when he was old enough to drive, he had to be home at 12:30. Once in awhile if he wanted to be later, he would call me. That was all I asked. He loved me and respected me enough to be considerate. He knew I would be waiting up for him.

He was always into sports. Sports helped discipline him a lot. It was school, sports, supper, homework, and bed. If they keep busy enough, they don't have time to get into trouble.

He had to do his homework. Once he had a homework project, and he procrastinated and let it slide. I asked him about it, and he said, "It's not finished, but I can do it in school tomorrow." And I said, "No, you are finishing it tonight and when you finish it you can go to bed. Homework that should be done at night is to be done at night. You can re-study the next day in school, but you can't leave your homework till the next day."

It got to be three o'clock in the morning, and I would not let him go to sleep. And I stayed up to make sure he did it. It was torture on both of us. I had one eye open and one eye closed, but I was determined to teach him a lesson. Needless to say, he never did that again.

He was not allowed out hanging around on the streets or the pizza parlor or the soda joints. Fortunately, he had mostly nice friends, but every once in awhile there would be one or two who were a bad influence on him. I told him to stay the hell away from them, that if you hang out with a bad crowd it will be your loss. You can be social with them in school, but you can't hang out with them. There was one girlfriend who was a real pain in the neck. She was fifteen going on thirty-five. She would call at all hours—even after midnight. She was ridiculous, and I told him so. I didn't forbid him to see her, but I told him what I thought. Fortunately it only lasted a year.

Of course, kids want to try things—cigarettes, beer—that's normal. And I said, "Sure, try it at home, but don't let me see you hanging around doing it." He experimented, but I made sure he didn't overdo it. He and his friends might drink a six pack in the yard in the summer, or I'd offer him a glass of wine with dinner, but he couldn't overdo it or make it a habit. When he was just sixteen, one of my cousins got married up in Massachusetts, and he was at the wedding. All the older guys were giving him different drinks, and he drank them because he was trying to keep up with them. He got so sick he'll never forget it. I said, "Well, you won't do that again will you?". But he was with his family, and he did it with us, and we were there to take care of him.

He tried cigarettes, but he didn't like them. I never smoked; I thought it was disgusting. And he looked up to me. There was a lot of dope in the school, and I told him to stay away from dope. And I'm sure he never even tried pot. He saw kids freaking out, and he had no interest in doing it.

I tried to set a good example for him. I taught him how to save money, how to make money. He always had summer jobs. He mowed lawns, he chopped wood, he did odd jobs in the neighborhood. The money was for his own spending money. I made sure he had everything he needed, but I wanted him to earn his own money so he'd know how to handle it. The last three years of high school he was saving money for college—he would bring me home his check, and I'd put it in the bank.

I taught him good manners and how to treat a woman. I didn't want him to be like his father. I taught him to treat a woman like I would like to be treated. He's thoughtful, kind, and considerate—that's the way a man should be brought up. He helped around the house. I taught him how to cook, and he likes cooking and baking.

I think children should be brought up in a religion. That way they have guidance. Craig went to sunday school, he was confirmed and went to church and Youth Fellowship. It's good to have youth be together in a religion and do social things. He made good friends through the church, nice kids, from good families.

I was strict, but he knew what I told him was for his own good. All my pushing was for the future, and it worked. Craig and I were physically affectionate. He was so much fun to be with. I wanted to be with him. I enjoyed every year, including the teenage years. We always did things together. I learned how to play golf and taught him. We also took karate together which was super. We each earned three belts. We used to practice at home—we'd spar and things. That was fun. We saved our money and went to Mexico for two weeks. And we had a fantastic time. Everybody thought we were brother and sister. I made sure his life wasn't a bore.

I made sure he had plenty of outlets. You have to work, you have to eat, you have to pay bills, but you have to do other things too. So I would take him a million places; to New York, to museums. I wanted to show him how the world lives. I made up my mind that I loved him and wanted him from the beginning and that I would devote my life to him till he was eighteen. And I did.

HANK

"I try not to use guilt to control them, but I do show them that they do all these great things and I do all the work."

Hank is a soft spoken, elegant mathematician whose wife, Mary, suddenly walked out on him and his two children. Hank found himself now mother and father to Philip in kindergarten and Kristen in 7th grade. His life alone with the children parallels that of many deserted women: the overwhelming demands of being a single parent, making money, meeting children's emotional and physical needs, keeping house. Although Hank's daughter Kristen is a great "success" and their relationship is good, this was not accomplished without pain and struggle.

At first I was flustered with running the house and preparing the meals because they weren't of an age where they could be of much help. I really only got Kristen into the meals when she insisted on being a vegetarian. We've gone through a year of the vegetarian thing, so she makes one or two meals a week, but before that I think I did too much. I found myself just going and going and going. They would only really help with housework and chores, but not with meals.

Now we have it running smoothly except once in a while I still feel like I do too much. Then I go through a thing where I show them, "Look, today I did this, this, and this. I wanted to do these nice things, but I didn't get a chance to do them." I try not to use guilt to control them, but I do show them that they did all these great things and I did all the work. So then they realize that, and for a week or two they're O.K. I expect certain things of Kristen, but I find I have to ask, and I resent that. So things just tend to slide. When I ask, she'll do it.

She's very preoccupied with school, and that's one of my dilemmas. I want her to do well in school, but sometimes I think she uses that as an excuse. She'll go a whole weekend doing mostly schoolwork and very little helping me around the house. I do expect more of Kristen, but I think it's because she's older. She can turn it around. She'll say, "Well, since I'm older, I would like more privileges or a bigger allowance." And she does get these things. She stays out later and she has more money. So going with that, she should contribute more to the family.

For me a problem with having the kids is also the socializing—of being able to go out. I guess I don't let myself go out as much as a bachelor would, and I don't have women come to my house overnight. I'm able to leave for the evening and leave Kristen and Philip together. I've always done that, but not for overnight. And I haven't really met someone to come live with me.

Men are asked this all the time—you go to the singles groups, and you meet a lot of women with two or three children, and they are looking for a man to help them out and to become part of the family. I'm looking for the same thing. There are times when what I need socially makes me so desperate that I feel I shouldn't have the kids. Even though I feel very proud of what I've done with them, maybe it's time for a change.

I don't dump my emotional problems on Kristen, but my life is wrapped up totally in hers so what I am going through pertains to her. My stability affects the kids. Sometimes, I have to fake that stability. Mary, my ex-wife, is under some pressure not to spend time with the kids. This fellow that she's living with has her on a very tight leash. It's better lately, but a year or two ago it was really bad. Kristen was very unhappy about it. She thought her mother didn't go shopping with her, didn't express an interest in her, and so she was looking for me to find someone to hang around with her. She was always talking to me about the different women I was seeing, what she thought of this one, what she thought of that one. And I really didn't care. I'd say, "Kristen, it's not for you. It's my life."

Mary was missing during those important years for her. Kristen was looking to me to be the strong leader, emotionally stable, so I did fake it a lot of times and cry after she went to bed. At first this was good for me because it gave me some total involvement. But I can see now that I should get away from it. Of course Kristen will be going to college soon and that will be a new stage.

Kristen had a rough time at first in high school. She was so unfriendly to the other kids. She wanted to transfer to a private school, but we couldn't afford it. I kept telling her to be a little more active and to reach out to people. Finally she got on a team, then on the yearbook, and now she has loads of friends and is very happy.

There have been several boy friends. She could probably have any boy she wants—she seems to be able to control it. She was going out with a boy for a while who I thought was beneath her—in terms of what he wanted in life, his conversation—his grammar wasn't correct. But he had a nice car, and she liked that. And if I had made a big fuss about it, it might have made him more attractive to her. But he just dropped out of her life. She somehow managed to stop the whole thing.

Kristen is not active sexually. That's just the way she is. That's going to be something for college. My rule for her is that she's not supposed to be alone at a boy's house. I stick to that rule. I say, "Well, you may hate me now, but someday you'll think I was right." When she goes out at night, she says what time she'll be back. We sort of negotiate it. Actually, I have a certain amount of jealousy when she goes out. She's got a lot of nice friends, and off she goes, and I'm home alone with Philip.

The main problem is that she focuses on herself too much.

She's very self centered. Fortunately, I've talked to other parents, and it's something to do with the teenage years; their own development is the most important thing to them. Right in the middle of some discussion or when Philip is talking she'll say something that just pertains to her—about college or something that has happened to her. I find that hard.

There are horrible things happening to me. I'm quite lonely, and things go wrong in my life, and she doesn't seem to notice what's going on with me. She counts on me for being there, and there's a meal on the table, and the house is fairly straight. So while I don't use her as a sympathizer, I try to tell her how things are with me.

I help her with her schoolwork. She has all A's, and she had the highest college board scores in the high school. She likes to have **things** worked out, she likes to know what's happening, but I tell her, "You can't always have things worked out. You think you have them worked out—and they're not." As I well know.

One thing people have pointed out to me is that I don't have specific ambitions for her. She has said to me, "What do you want me to be? What do you want me to do?" I say, "Nothing. I just want you to grow up and be happy, and you can pick out what you want to do." She used to say that was hard for her. It would have been easier if I had wanted her to do something. She could have either rebelled against it or just done it. It's not that I'm holding back, I really don't have anything particular in mind for her.

I said to my children recently, "What will you remember of your childhood? Will you remember the four of us, or will you remember growing up with me?" They were nervous. They didn't say anything. But I think Kristen will remember growing up with me. She has an inner gyroscope that will carry her through. I think I gave her that.

MOIRA

"We three truly are friends. We are a unit. . . . it's a unit that cannot be fractured, and I don't think it ever will be."

Intense, intelligent, and creative, Moira is struggling to bring up two teenagers in the moneyed, fast moving society of Los Angeles, California. She is a writer/producer, widely traveled, has been married and divorced twice and is the product of a strict English/French upbringing. Her views on child raising reflect the interesting dichotomy in her own nature. She will not tolerate impertinence or "that ghastly rock and roll," yet she encourages Jason to have an affair with one of her friends.

Moira is idealistic about the quality of the work that she does and consequently makes very little money. Her children are supportive of this and of her search for a good man. She emphasizes the honesty and friendship that characterizes her relationship with Jason and Noelle yet adds that she's reluctant to burden them with too much and that she's not afraid to be the authority when it's necessary.

My son is now sixteen, my daughter just turned fifteen. I've been raising them alone since they were seven and five, with a brief marriage in between. I have a great deal of love and affection for them. They are remarkable children.

I don't have the kinds of complaints about them that I hear about other children. I have an enormous amount of respect for them, particularly my son. There are almost times when I learn from Jason. He is a very intelligent boy, a very rounded person, and he has an enormous sense of humor. I also have implicit trust in them. I always have.

My kids are gorgeous, they're heaven, they're fun, they're my friends. They are enormously supportive of me. I had them when I was very young; I was thirty-eight last week. Being single in a rather strange society—as it is in Los Angeles—there are moments when I'm certainly crumbling. They are enormously supportive of my decisions.

I'm a writer. I'm not going to make very much money as such. Neither of them have come down on me and said, "But why don't you take a nine to five job like all the other people we know and get more sensible?" They are most supportive of my need to be a writer. In and of itself, that is terribly valuable. Both times I was married I didn't get that kind of support from their father nor my second husband, which I get from these kids.

Things have changed since their adolescence. My daughter has just turned fifteen. She's a very sexual little creature and beginning to become aware of her sexuality. This scares me because I now realize her vulnerability. In spite of all the years of upholding women's lib and treating them the same, etc. etc., I do find the double standard creeping in. I can't help it. It's more a matter of wanting to protect Noelle. She is a different person from Jason. She's much more vulnerable, more sensitive, more prone to be hurt. I know she's going to have at least eight broken hearts in the next five years. And so my honesty is becoming a little tempered with their adolescence. I am fearful for my daughter; there is that need to protect.

The principles I have for child-rearing and the application are not always the same thing. The ideal as I see it is to be able to be very honest and share things. One can't. When you're leading your own life, there are times when you don't want them to know all that much about it. Some things are private. I tend to keep private now my emotions regarding men, my sex life. Yet if my children don't like a man, he's out. They're a very good barometer for me, and I can't proceed with any relationship unless they like him. They're usually right. They've never been wrong yet.

When I become depressed, I try and hide it. I think it's too scary for them. Being adolescents themselves, they really would take on the responsibility of wanting to make it better for me when they couldn't. They do have a lot of pressure already without a father around and without very much money around. So to show them my extreme depression would, I think, be extremely unfair. So I might say, "I'm feeling down, quiet; I'm not feeling so good." But I wouldn't share the depths of how bad I'm feeling.

We're very honest about money. I say, "Put those lights out unless you want to take out shares in General Electric." There is this sort of caring, there is the caring of not throwing away food . . . the normal household economies. Instead of having a cleaning lady, they have undertaken to accomplish what's on the list. It is firmly abided by. They get paid. And if they don't do certain jobs, money gets taken off. Money is given to them for that job whether they're rude or not. They have earned that money. It's a contract. They're the "cleaning lady." They cook. Now Jason even drives and can do the shopping if absolutely necessary. I'd rather the money went into their pockets than into the cleaning lady's pockets.

They are different. I have an extraordinarily tidy son and an extremely untidy daughter. I have had to discipline my children, of course. One of the things I find myself doing is putting guilt trips on them. It's very insidious. I've been recently realizing I've been doing what my mother did to me. When all else fails and I can't get through, I'll find myself doing a guilt trip. I came home the other night and said to Jason, "Cook dinner." "I can't Mom, I have five hours of homework." I was exhausted that night. I had three thousand things to do and instead of saying very straight, "Look, I have also got six hours of stuff to do, let's share it," I said, "Don't worry. . . ." I did an enormous guilt trip with him which he didn't accept, for he's very healthy in that way. For out and out discipline with Jason, I refuse to let him use the car, but he doesn't seem to need discipline too much. He does little that is bad.

Both children loathe cigarettes. Drinking, I'm not remotely worried about it. I happen to have two rather extraordinary kids in this area. They hate drugs, they hate alcohol, they hate cigarettes; they hate me smoking. Jason did take grass once and had a very bad experience, and I was delighted. He was thirteen, and he's never touched it since. Noelle certainly won't take drugs, I know what sort of a person she is. A lot of that is that I also don't take drugs.

I'm not worried about sexual promiscuity in Noelle. I don't think I'll even have to worry as she gets older. With the double standard, I wonder, "Is there such a thing as sexually promiscuous sixteen year old boy?" I wish Jason would have a sexual experience and get it done with. I've been trying to help with a friend of mine who is thirty-three and who adores him. I have been actively pushing this, the young boy with the older woman. I'd love for him to have his first sexual experience in this way.

One of my big scares in raising adolescents is herpes. This is really becoming a very big scare for me. It's also scary for them, too. We discuss it very openly. Whether they are keeping things from me, I don't know. I don't think they are. Still, there must be areas. . . . They'd have to be very strange to tell me everything.

There is one thing that repeats over and over again: we three truly are friends. We are a unit. We do have fights—very loud, angry fights. Nevertheless, it's a unit that cannot be fractured and I don't think it ever will be.

My family makeup is more like brothers and sisters because I was so young when I started. I never really see myself in an authoritative type role. However, I'm aware I'm a parent. Noelle recently said, "You're not my friend." I remember saying, "If I have to sacrifice a friendship in order to be the authority right now, I'll do that." I knew that I wouldn't really have to sacrifice the friendship because that argument was going to last for about two or three days, and that was that. It wasn't a particularly important one. At this stage I really haven't had to use very heavy discipline. There have been things like, "You're grounded. You can't take the car tonight." What causes this is impertinence. I can't stand impertinence. More than a fresh mouth, it's rather a tone. My son is a very intellectual boy, and he can tie people up in intellectual knots. And when he comes with an intellectual tone which reduces me to being an absolute simpleton, I haven't yet dealt with it in a wise fashion. I absolutely can't abide the impertinence. That's one of the first things I'll discipline them for. The things like tidying up, which drive you crazy, you can get round those things. You can make a straight demand, "I want that room done in half an hour." End of conversation. They'll start hedging, "But, I can't, I've got to make a phone call." Finally they do the chore. I've found it extremely important to follow through. If I make a threat, or whatever you call it, I have to follow through no matter how I feel about it because I usually want to change it.

I think one of the things that makes me terribly sad is that I get a very deep feeling of having denied them a full family by not having a father around. I really do feel I'm taking away a strong part of their birthright. I think part of them resents me too. We do make efforts. I said a few months ago, "OK, there's a new rule around here. Every Sunday afternoon we're going to get together, regardless. The three of us will be together, whether we have friends in or whether we're going sailing or whatever we're going to do, we're going to do together." It only works to a certain extent because I'm just as moody as they are. I don't follow through on it as much as I'd like. I find it's a weakness in me, not them. Because I think that if I said, "We are going to a park, or we're going to play tennis together," they'd do it.

I'm not decrying America. I love this country. I've chosen

to live here, but they did spend their formative years in England, and that may have had something to do with their way of being. They came here with a different sense of values. However, what they gained from America was wonderful: they gained the freedom of expression which British children are not really given. But what they got from a British—their initial—upbringing was a very different sense of values and also an obedience which I don't find that prevalent in American children. My inability to not be able to abide impertinence might be a give-away as to my European background. I will tolerate other things which annoy me, but impertinence is bad for them and for me. So, I am somewhat aware of having taught my children manners. I make sure they ring up and thank people or write to people and thank them. I'm constantly being told by people that they are extraordinarily polite. They're not angels at all, but they are polite to people. They are sensitive to people who do good things to them.

My son is a high achiever, but my daughter has not quite such a high self-esteem as I'd like her to have. She measures herself a great deal against him, and he's bugging the holy hell out of me by not being as supportive of her as he should be because he has it within him to support her a great deal more. He's sixteen. He's got a very attractive, beautiful fifteen year old sister. They fight; he loves her enormously, but he could be giving her a great deal more. Noelle's self-esteem is not high enough. She's a girl, that may be part of it, and she has also watched my struggles.

They have been in private school for quite a long time, but I've just taken my daughter out and put her in public school. I ran out of money, and the scholarship ran out. Jason has gone through one of the very best schools in California on a gigantic scholarship for the last four years on academic ability and his athletic ability and is going to Brown University in the fall.

I'm consciously, very consciously, trying *not* to do what my mother did in raising me. My mother was extraordinarily volatile, very unreasonable and irrational. She also used to slap me. I don't hit my children at all. It was a conscious decision on my part when I was young. My mother is a very strong influence in my life. She is very manipulative, a strong, forceful personality. She has not stopped treating me very much the same as she treated me when I was thirteen with an enormous amount of love but not very much liking. My mother paid me the very first compliment of my adult life recently. She said over the phone, because it would have been hard to say face to face, "I want to tell you how I admire you, and that your children are your friends, and they really are your friends." I asked the children later what prompted her to say that. Apparently she had come into their bedrooms and was trying to persuade them to do something to persuade me to do something, manipulating me through them. And they said no. So she realized that she's really hurt two close friends of mine. There's no similarity in the way I raise my kids. I think I've succeeded in overcoming my mother's method, and it's very important that I do because my mother was not a good mother.

When I remarried they were young. I think that they were possibly relieved that Mummy had someone to look after her which really in that case meant them. My ex-husband's a very kind, gentle person but unfortunately given to irrational fits of bad temper. During the entire four years of marriage, I felt like the meat in between the sandwich. I was trying to keep the peace. He loved them but I was always aware they were not his children. And he needed more peace; he needed more tidiness. He never had his own children. It was exhausting. But I absolutely do not think the children contributed to the divorce. It was Paul and I that went wrong. I think being a step-father is not an easy thing, and being a mother and re-marrying with two fairly young kids is not that easy either. The children took the divorce rather differently. Jason was much more pragmatic about it, he felt it coming. Noelle hid a great deal of her feelings. But once again, they were support-ive of me.

My children feel that I fuck up with men. Recently, this summer, my children were on holiday with their father who lives overseas. While they were away, I wrote to them saying I'd met this wonderful man. I didn't go overboard and say he was splendid. I told them I liked him very much. Noelle wrote back straight away saying, "Don't do it again, don't jump right in as you usually do and fall in love and get hurt." So now I have a daughter who is looking critically at my relationships with men and I think is not altogether approving. In many ways, Jason is the man of the house. I think he would love to feel that Mum is being taken care of. Mum is not taking care of herself very well financially and in many ways emotionally. I've raised them, we're in our own place. Everything's fine, but it could be a helluva lot better.

My children are an enormous joy to me. Even when they are a burden and they are expensive and I have to go and pick them up twenty miles away and I'd rather not. There's no way, not for a fraction of my adult life, I have regretted having those two children. They're very aware of that. Even during arguments with the usual line of, "Well, why did you have me anyway?," I will say to them that "I love you." I think my children are enormously aware of that love I have for them, and I'm very certain I have tremendous love for them.

I have certain values I have wanted to instill in my kids. One is that while money is important in our society, it's not as important as Los Angeles would have you think. The school Jason goes to is a very moneyed school, and the kids are all given Porsches when they turn sixteen. Now Jason is dying for the day when he puts down his *own* money for his own car. I don't want to make him sound like a saint, but I have done this consciously through our conversations.

Another value I would like to instill is a kind of sensitivity at an age when they are both interested in the opposite sex. With Jason I say, "Allright, you want to fuck. But you must take into account that this is a human being who is sensitive, as sensitive as your sister, who probably like your sister, spent an hour getting dressed, not knowing what to wear. Be kind. Be sensitive." With Noelle, she sees the agonies her brother goes through just having to pick up the phone and make a date and. . . . "My God Mom, how am I going to tell her she's got to pay her own way into the film?" So Noelle is already seeing that in her brother.

I am also trying to make them see the joyful, positive side of life. So the car breaks down. It didn't crash. It's as much for my benefit as it is for them. It's the old bottle is it half empty or is it half full syndrome. I'm trying to make them see the bottle as half full. Teaching always goes on.

My children will ask for advice, not so much now as they used to. They are more autonomous, but Noelle will say, "Should I tell my friend she's fat?" That's in a way, a pretty important question because she's dealing with sensitivity to other people. I tell her not to tell her friend, just joke with her perhaps but certainly not tell her she's obese. I go to my kids for advice too. Recently I discussed a job possibility with them because this is their lives too. I took their advice, "Don't take the job." But had they said, "Try it for a week," I think I possibly would have. I believe in being as honest with my kids as possible if it's something they can do something about. Otherwise it's better left unsaid. If they can be helpful and they can take that on, great, why not? Good for them, good for me. I feel very blessed that I do have two very special human beings. They have qualities that do not come from me. I don't think they come from their father. Perhaps this hard life has been helpful to them. Maybe it's the old saying that adversity teaches. There have been studies that have proved it. They have had a very rich life. They have traveled a great deal. They are richer than a lot of their friends who are moneyed.

I have tried to give them a great love of nature since they were very young. They have an enormous love for it. One of the reasons Jason wants to go to the east coast is the seasons, the trees, the green. Noelle is exactly the same. That's wonderful because that's free and always very soothing to the soul. I also have surrounded them with books. I encourage them to read. I've made a conscious effort to give them good music. I couldn't believe that my son went out a few years ago and bought his first Vivaldi record. We share music. We go to the theatre. I will not have that ghastly rock and roll when I'm in the house. That doesn't mean they don't play it when I'm out. But I do think my kids will just obey me, and that's that. Now whether this is going to last, I don't know, but I think it will.

I really do believe that some part of parenting is luck. I've seen some tremendous parents with rotten kids, and vice versa. My two both happen to be good. The child's individuality has to come into very strong account. You can't take all the credit and all the blame for your children. I'm certainly not doing it. I refuse to accept all the blame and all the credit. The credit I take very little for because I often look at my kids and say, "Where did you come from?" I didn't instill certain things they have.

My kids have shot up recently and as I mentioned before are becoming very sexual. I'm very aware that my son is an extraordinarily good-looking and very sexual young man. I will not play those games that I see happening between mother and son, which are dangerous. I'm talking about a specific society like Los Angeles. This has got to be peculiar to that type of society where people are a little more experiment oriented. I have witnessed a great deal of flirtation between mother and son. There are times when I go to Jason and say, "Dance with me." But I'm not flirting; I'm really being a friend. But I have seen that line crossed a bit, not from the son but from the mother. That is something I will not do. Whereas I used to race around the house with very little clothing on, I won't do it in front of Jason now. I will wear underpants and a T-shirt but not a see through bra anymore. That's going to place stress on him which he doesn't need right now. I'm still young. He's a very sexual human being. It's subtle, but it's a responsibility I must take on. His friends are around a great deal. Hulking, great seventeen, eighteen year old kids. I can no longer lie in the sun without my bikini top on as I did just two, three years ago. Whether it's a deference, a respect, a modesty for him, I don't know. But I think it's important. It's somewhere in there a respect between a man and a woman, respecting their sexuality. And I don't think there's been a stage where I'm not aware of the fact that I really do respect these people—my daughter and my son.

MICHAEL

"They way they were brought up by us with a reasonable approach coupled with their own good judgement . . . as well as a lot of luck and a lot of love are the reasons for their turning out so well and being successful."

Originally a big city policeman who worked nights and went to school days to earn a master's degree from a rigorous Catholic college, Michael now teaches social studies, criminology and law in a rural high school. He moved to the country because he felt the economy and atmosphere would be easier and better for raising a family. He has six successful happy children, a colleague of his describes them as "Remarkable," whom he and his wife raised in the model of their own rather strict Irish Catholic upbringing.

The children's lives are diverse and interesting. Francis, who specializes in architectural design, lives prosperously and happily in Alabama with his wife and daughter. Patricia and Sean have bought a house together on the west coast; he manages a retail department store, she runs a busy restaurant. Ellen is a florist and a mother, and Mary Beth, a communications major, is involved in drama and her college radio station.

Michael himself is an active man with many interests. An avid bicyclist and swimmer, he's been involved in theatre, politics and many voluntary village organizations. Michael is unique in that he can't recall any major problems with six(!) children probably due to his consistency and solidity in everything he does and says.

My basic philosophy about child rearing was based on how I was raised. I grew up in the city, the oldest of six children. My mother worked part-time but was mostly a housewife. We went to Catholic schools and colleges. For a while I sent my children to Catholic schools in the city. Then when we moved to the country, we shifted the kids to the public schools mainly because we felt the public school program was a little broader: music lessons, art. My daughters, especially, were interested in music, and that was part of the reason for the shift.

We didn't really have a game plan, but both of us raised our children like our own parents raised us. We raised them in the religion. They went to church on Sunday and holy days. They were baptized, confirmed, and had religious instruction. They prayed at home. It wasn't overdone, but we were religious.

We had some rules for our children. We were not very strict with our teenagers. There were some guidelines: curfews, for example. As far as smoking went only one of our kids smoked; she smoked in high school, not at home. There wasn't really a problem with this. My kids were really very involved in activities. The oldest boys were into football, basketball and cross country. Two of the girls were musically and artistically inclined. Joyce was the third girl down, much more than anyone in the family, a real athlete. She was very big in basketball and field hockey. Mary Beth, our last child, now in college, gave a try at sports in high school and did rather well but didn't stay with it because she got into yearbooks, and the school paper. She was also a musician as well as very active in the theatre. All of them were fairly good students, average to good.

Mary Beth was in drama in school, in Knowland Hall (our community theatre). She has had many jobs and showed great energy for anything she did. She was always an active money earner. In college she is now getting involved in the radio station, is in the process of auditioning.

There was a good amount of family life. We would go into the city together, we'd travel. We'd visit relatives. We moved out of the city twenty-five years ago, and for the kids sake we'd do the tourist bit in the city. The kids were exposed to different things in the city, but here in the country, there were many benefits. For example, I got involved in the summer theatre, and so my kids could see whatever shows they wanted. I was the manager, and the fringe benefits were that they could see the play and that they could also get involved in the theatre life.

I was usually pleased with my kids' friends. They were quite popular. I always felt they exercised good judgment and felt little need to restrict them. They were easy-going kids. We had few big problems. No drunk driving. No one was arrested.

Most of the time my wife was home, but ten years ago she did start to work summer jobs. With the theatre and with my teaching I was mostly always working. Recently in the summers I've been taking it more easy, only tutoring and doing some real estate work.

We all worked for money. We aren't rich as a family of eight on a teacher's salary. We didn't give them allowances, but when they needed money they were given it. They also had good paying jobs and paid for what they could. But weekly stipends, we never got into that.

Our kids were pretty obedient. They came home on time, generally speaking. We had our times of crises, our times of yelling at each other. Our kids were sensible kids. Perhaps they learned good judgment from their relatives, their parents. The way they were brought up by us with a reasonable approach, coupled with their good judgment and their sensible approach as well as a lot of luck and a lot of love are the reasons for their turning out so well and being so successful.

Being a fair human being with people you run into and have contact with is terribly important. I always felt it was important to provide them with this value. The kids all had jobs, mostly weekend and summer jobs which provided all of us with insight into human nature which we would share at the table. We always ate dinner together. This was part of our general routine. My wife and I tried to go to church together. Both of us had had a strong religious upbringing. During their childhood and teen years we tried to instill in them sensitivity to other people, a certain sense of self-esteem and pride. We stressed manners at the table and in relationship with other people: respect for the elderly, respect for everyone. They learned by example from us. They saw us trying to be just with others.

My children all went to school where I taught, and what effect this had on them I may never know because I've never inquired and don't know if I will. It probably had something to do with their behavior, how they conducted their own lives and also how they saw me. They probably had a much better picture of their father, seeing him both at work and at home. It probably restricted them as well. I never felt they resented my having to be one of their teachers. Actually only two of my children ended up taking courses from me. They did very well, and it was very satisfying to me.

I'm not the sort of parent who lets it all hang out. I didn't show my emotions very easily. I expressed anger if I felt it. Sometimes I think my wife was sensitive to my anger welling into an explosion and would put the family on alert.

I didn't have long-range plans for my children. I did want them to try and prepare themselves with some kind of college preparation and if they felt they could handle it go all the way for a four year degree. If possible I would help them financially. All of them did go but not all to four year colleges. My hope was that upon completion of whatever education they chose they would be able to support themselves, their families. I have tried to lean on my kids a bit to show them how important it is to better oneself through education. My children all make good money, especially my grown ones.

My expectations were general, but they knew I wanted

them to have some direction in life. I wasn't completely laissez faire about everything they did, but I will say that I didn't expect them to follow in my footsteps. They could do their own thing. They seemed to accept their responsibilities and worked hard. They seem to be doing that now in their adult life.

Relatives have been very important in our family life. My wife's family, mine. My mother is still alive. She re-married after my father died. There were relatives in the city, and there were relatives near by in the country. So my children would see these relatives fairly often. People would either visit us, or we'd go visit them. Cousins here, cousins there. They learned from their contacts from their relatives. I've always felt confident that their judgment was good partly due to the exposure to different people. And exposure to their own mother who was with them a great deal more than I. I was out of the house a great deal working. I sometimes wish I had been able to be at home more with the family. My children confided more in my wife than me. They came to her for advice more than they did to me.

The kids had chores to do of course. After they left I realized how much the kids had been doing in the way of lawn cutting, garden work, helping around the house because now it was all left for us to do, just the two of us. I get someone to do some of the work a few hours a week so I can enjoy biking and swimming which are two sports I've gotten into since the kids have grown up.

I don't regret anything that has gone down. I don't think I would have done anything differently. When I think of our move from the city I know I missed the active life of the city, but I knew it was a better life for the children in the country. But because of my job in the summer theatre and our contacts there, there was an opportunity for exposure to the fine arts, people, culture—things that are pretty commonplace in the city. I would have preferred to see my kids go to four year schools. But that was carried over from my time. And nowadays I don't feel that is a formula that works for everybody. I feel I've changed in that respect. I don't feel it to be that important to go to college for four years.

We are a Catholic family, but that in no way influences my expectations for their married life. I'm pleased with whom my kids have so far married. In fact, two of my children didn't marry Catholics. That isn't a big thing to me. Twenty-five years have gone by since the Catholic church was telling us that mixed marriages are out. Things have changed, I have changed. It would be absurd to think that mixed marriages were out of the question. I am happy if my kids are happy. My grandchildren who are living in the South were baptized in the Catholic Church, but they are going to Baptist Bible School now. I don't resent this at all.

As my kids are growing, family relationships have solidified more and more. Mary Beth and her sister Ellen have become closer and closer over the last years. And between myself and my kids my relationship is a real source of pleasure. This is probably due to the fact that all along the family has had close relationships.

We have been very lucky with our children. They show respect for others. They seem very solid. They seem really rather spectacular. I really enjoy my children. I enjoyed having them, but I notice I'm enjoying them much more now than I did in the past. I over-involved myself while they were growing up in town politics, in work. I got elected on a write-in vote which my kids helped me with, which is sort of remarkable. We won! My theatre took up a lot of good-weather time—sixty hours a week. I wasn't able to spend as much time in the home life. I was more of an absentee father. Now I'm less involved in things like church, veterans, village, fire department—I got out of the fire department recently after twenty-five years of service. So the last few years have been less frantic, and I've been able to be around them more. We have gone out to discos together to dance. Occasionally we'll go out to eat and have a few drinks together. Or I'll go biking with them now. Mary Beth and I went biking a few days ago, and Ellen and I went out to dinner recently together.

The only big problem I might have had was that I was not at home terribly much. But if I think about it that might not have changed things much because being teenagers they too would have been out of the house a lot doing their jobs. All I know is they seem to have a lot of fun with their father and vice versa. I am very proud of my kids, very satisfied with what they have become, happy with who they have become. I feel very lucky and thankful.

HELEN

"You have to put a great deal of faith in kids. I always trusted them. I never doubted their ability."

Helen and George are "typical" middle class Americans. Good citizens, church-going republicans, George worked as a salesman, Helen a housewife. Their three children grew up in a modest suburb and attended public school. All were athletic, musical, popular, and excellent students. All went to college. Alex is a geologist, Wendy a medical technologist, Jim dropped out of college and is an accomplished woodworker and musician. The children are independent, hard working adults, leading interesting lives. They are fond of their parents and visit them often. Helen emphasizes continuity and closeness—meals together, music together, church together, leisure activity together. But most notable in her story is the self-fulfilling prophecy: "We become what we are expected to become." Though her children grew up in the troubled decades of the 60's and 70's, she never expected trouble and never got it. She never doubted the validity of her values and her children, unlike so many others, never did either.

My kids all went to church. I insisted on that. And I not only that, but I insisted that my husband and I set an example. I didn't believe in sending them off to Sunday school and us reading the paper or staying in bed later. We went too, every Sunday. That would have been hypocritical to send them off and not go ourselves. They had seven years of perfect attendance in Sunday school, and they all sang in the choir.

We had their two grandmothers living here during their teenage years, and they were marvelous. They were never too tired to pay attention to the children, they were always very tolerant of them, very loving to them. The kids loved having them here. They learned a lot from each other. And it was really a help to me. There was always someone there when we went out, though we didn't go out much. My kids were never left alone.

I remember one time Jim was planning a party with his high school friends, and one of the girl's mothers asked me at a school meeting, "Do you know this party's taking place?" And I said, "Indeed I do." She said, "Will you be there?" And I said, "I definitely will." I didn't blame her for being concerned. She had a daughter, and she didn't know me. Being so active in the school I was able to know the parents of my children's friends. When they were invited to a party, I knew the home they were going to, where they lived, what the parents were like.

I never worked outside of the house, but I was active in the P.F.A. (P.T.A.). Even though George worked six days a week, he was very active in sports and helped coach the baseball team. When the boys were about thirteen, the big thing was soap box races and cars, and George spent a whole winter in his spare time at nights in the cellar with the boys building those soap box racers. He did a lot of things with the kids and so did I. We went to all their sports events. We took an interest in everything they did. We always planned family vacations.

George took a large part in disciplining the boys. He never struck them, but one time Alex was rude to me, he was fresh, he snapped at me, and George slapped him right in the face. I'll always remember that. George was a wonderful father. He really was. He was understanding of them. During the Vietnam War I remember George giving Alex some advice when it looked inevitable that Alex would be brought in, and Alex didn't know what to do about joining. So George advised him to go into ROTC. It seemed apropos in view of all that was going on. George said, "Go in and be somebody and join ROTC." Which Alex did. He took his advice and got a commission.

The boys and George played music together. Jim played the saxophone, and Alex and George played the trumpet. They used to play together almost every night sometimes to the detriment of dinner. They used to sing and harmonize mostly around Christmas. You know, "It's beginning to look a lot like Christmas" and all that sort of thing. The neighbors would come in and listen.

We had rules. They had curfews. They had to be in at certain hours. They had to be here for meals on time. Dinner was at 6 o'clock. I emphasized manners without laying down any hard and strict rules. There was no television during meals. I hear of a lot of kids eating dinner in front of the television, but I thought that dinner was a good place to have conversation and socialize—and the grandmothers ate with us too.

One time Alex was playing football, and he had been to some football affair, and the coach was there and his wife, and it seems like Alex was drinking before he went to this thing, and he was rude to the coach's wife. The coach called up and wanted to meet with George and talk to him about it. They did meet, and George straightened things out. I never asked them what was said.

Oh, and another time, Alex was out at a party or somewhere, and we got a call about 1:30 in the morning from a friend of his that he was with saying that Alex's car had broken down and he was going to stay at his house all night. And I said, "That's fine. But I want him home at 9 o'clock tomorrow morning to go to church." And Alex was home the next morning. Of course it really wasn't the car at all—he'd been drinking too much.

When Wendy went with Bob, I didn't like the idea of her going with one boy so much. I thought she should spread herself out a bit. Not that I objected to him. He wasn't a bad kid. I never forbid her to go out with him, but I told her what I thought.

I wasn't too subtle when I didn't care for someone. Like I never cared for Wendy's friend Stacy. Wendy knew it, and Stacy sensed it. I thought Stacy was too free with boys. I thought she was a bad influence on Wendy, and I made no bones about it. I showed my dislike for Stacy. It naturally came out. But I never wanted Wendy to feel her friends weren't welcome. So Stacy remained a friend of Wendy's. I never talked to Wendy about sex. She never asked me. But if she had, I would have been reluctant to answer, to talk about it. The boys never asked about it either. Maybe because I was older than most of the mothers—I was forty-three when I had Wendy.

I never had to push them with their homework. They always got excellent grades, but I never remember telling them they had to. They seemed very self motivated. But I wasn't a pusher in general. I didn't want to push them to overachieve. I wanted them to work at their own levels. There was a time when Alex was playing baseball and he was taking French and he wasn't doing very well. He was kept off the team for a week. And Alex said, "But I hate French." And the coach said, "We don't care if you hate it. Just pass it." I don't think I would have done that.

I hoped my children would be college educated because I had had that advantage. One of my heartbreaks was when Jim dropped out of college because he had such great potential. I tried to talk him out of it, but I didn't threaten him. I never threatened them with anything.

I smoke. But thank goodness my kids never took it up— they didn't follow me. I never even had to talk to them about it. They never wanted to.

They had chores. George worked Saturdays so Alex and Jim mowed the lawn and did the trimming. They did it with no problems. I never had to urge them. They just did it.

Summers they worked to earn money. Jim worked on construction jobs, and they used to help around in the neighborhood—little odd jobs. Jim also used to sing in a quartet and earned $5 a Sunday. They had allowances. George used to give them so much every week, but I don't remember what it was. They earned their own money though it didn't amount to that much. It didn't go toward college. It was just pin money to get along on—to go on dates and things like that.

I'm a very demonstrative person and so is George. He's very warm. George and I were loving toward each other in front of the kids, but we never discussed our personal lives or feelings. We never discussed money. They had what we could give them, with limitations.

You have to put a great deal of faith in kids. I always trusted them. I never doubted their ability. When they said they'd be home, I never doubted it. I always let them drive when I was in the car.

I had a very happy childhood myself, and I was very close to my parents, and this reflected on my children.

JOHN

"The necessary limits are fairly natural, they don't have to be imposed . . . or made up arbitrarily. Limits that are necessary are necessary because they are essential."

John is a professor of philosophy at a prestigious liberal arts college. He is interested in law and has been active in civil rights since his college days. He is married to a psychologist. Chris, eighteen, is their only child. Since Chris's infancy, John has assumed an active role in child raising. His wife has always worked, so it was necessary that all household responsibilities be shared.

Chris is a handsome, quiet boy, popular, athletic, an outstanding student. He is close to his parents, though at the time of this interview Chris was going through a period of separating from John, "establishing himself as an adult." John is glad of this, however, because he felt in early adolescence Chris was too dependent on him as a companion.

I think I helped raise Chris successfully. He does well in school. I influenced him to value that, also his interest in sports. Some of his sensitivities he probably picked up from me. I've contributed my sense of irony, a sense of humor, a certain awareness of inequality and unfairness. I always talked to him, engaged him in conversation, was always myself in front of him. I made a big effort to instill in him a suspicion of hucksterism on T.V. I was critical of things that I thought were tasteless drivel though I never censored anything he did.

I spent a lot of time with him. We watched T.V. together.

We discussed events, common experiences. We talked about my work; I've always tried to interest him in what I'm doing. We made sure he was in a good school in a good neighborhood with people that he would like.

We have rules for him in an ad hoc way, case by case. We tell him what time to come home since he's driving our car. He gets an allowance regularly, but I give him extra money if he has a good reason. I want him to look for a summer job this year, but I won't put pressure on him. I've been able to deal with him successfully without using a lot of pressure. He earns some money mowing lawns. He has chores around the house. He's encouraged to be home for dinner, and he usually is. If he isn't, he'll call. He's not allowed to drink and drive. He drinks a little, and he smokes dope—sometimes with us— and he's allowed to. He doesn't have to do it behind our back. He seems not to be inclined to smoke cigarettes. I told him I'd give him a thousand dollars if he didn't smoke by twenty-one. He remembers that and reminds me of it. We appreciate the fact that he's doing well in school and that he's responsible and responsive.

The trick to child raising is to try to relate to the child in such a way that you're influencing him or her to be as independent and as capable of becoming the person that he or she could become. There's an art to it in not overly indoctrinating or conditioning, yet at the same time, not being so permissive as to provide a totally unreal environment that would not be at all like the so called real world. I always felt there was some sort of Aristotelean mean between being overly directive and overly permissive and undirective. It was never necessary for me to use physical force in a punitive way.

On a certain scale I would be considered permissive, but it seemed to me that I was aware of what I was doing. I let him do almost anything providing it wasn't dangerous to him or to somebody else. The same limits apply to him as a teenager. We have a good enough understanding and relationship that there are not any serious problems. He knows our needs; he's involved with living with us. The necessary limits are fairly natural; they don't have to be imposed on him or made up arbitrarily. Limits that are necessary are necessary because they're essential. He's internalized our values, he respects us and our needs, he doesn't go to extremes. We've given him a lot of opportunities. We leave him alone for a few days at a time. Last summer, when we were away he had a fairly substantial beer party at the house. I found garbage cans filled with beer cars. I wasn't angry. I did the same kind of things at his age.

There was a period of time in early adolescence when he was too dependent on me for most of his needs. I was a little concerned and attempted to encourage him to make other friends. I insisted that he bring friends to the house. Now he remembers that well.

He has a girlfriend now; he's out of the house a lot with her and his other friends. He's very independent. He has a lot of things he likes to do by himself. He's fairly laconic with me these days, though he talks a lot to his mother. Right now he's reluctant to be too involved with me. But I'm not trying to combat it—it's a natural reaction. This is an evolutionary thing. He was much too dependent on me as a companion. He's finally gotten to the stage where his peers are much more important to him. I get the sense that it's not "cool," not "with it," to have too close a relationship with your parents. He's playing out this stage right now; needs to establish himself as an adult. It's not an irrevocable rift.

BARBARA

"I want her to make it, but I don't want her to sacrifice her whole being in the process."

There are two unique aspects to Barbara's story. The first is her strict, old world, Armenian background; her sheltered existence, her complete immersion in the Armenian culture. She attended Armenian schools and churches, lived in an all Armenian community. She is proud of her background; her house is filled with Armenian art and artifacts, but she has tried to modify the repressive aspects of her upbringing and to equip her children for modern times. The second aspect concerns her daughter Karen, who is a musical prodigy and has dedicated her life to her art. Barbara's task has been to encourage this gift while insuring a normal life for her daughter.

Barbara herself, is a stunningly beautiful woman, looking a bit like an athletic Sophia Loren. She is, in fact, a champion tennis player. She is married to a prosperous Armenian merchant much older than herself, who is also much more conservative in his views. Although she didn't have to work outside the home, she is a painter and a photographer. A woman of many interests and talents, she has tried to inculcate some of them in her children. Her son Thomas was salutatorian of his high school class, is a tennis pro, and attends a well known university where he studies computer engineering and maintains a near perfect scholastic average. Her daughter Karen, a senior in high school, has sung starring roles in operas since she was thirteen, is studying at Julliard and hopes to make it to the top.

I had my children when I was very young, very immature, but I did know I had shortcomings in my own growing up environment that I wanted to overcome. I knew that I wanted my children to have a lot of exposure and direction. I took them to museums, enrolled them in special programs. But I was growing at that time too, along with them. I started developing a lot of interests, and this fed their interests. They emulate me and look up to me. Their father is a wonderful father and provider, but he's been passive concerning their upbringing; he's a bit of a workaholic. It's largely been left up to me to guide them. And of course, I never had to work to earn money so I had a lot of time to spend with them.

One of my interests was music. It has always been a very important part of my life. Music was playing in the house all day long. I started my son on music lessons when he was very young. He didn't like it but Karen, when she went along with me for his lessons, was so stimulated; she obviously loved every bit of it. She took an interest immediately. When I saw this I began voice and piano lessons for her. She soon became a featured soloist in various church choirs; she played Amahl in Menotti's opera on tour when she was thirteen. At that point, we started to drive her all the way into New York every weekend for lessons at Julliard. It's an extremely long drive and very time consuming. She lost a certain amount of her growing up period, a lot of her friends. By the time she got home on Sunday night she was out of the mainstream of social life.

This year I finally put a stop to it. I felt we needed to take the pressure off—it's too much for a child. The competition in the music world is incredible. There's so much else in the world. I want to encourage her music, yet I want her to socialize too. Last year there was zilch socially for her. I want to change that. Last Sunday I had a dinner party for ten of her young friends. I insisted she stop practicing at a decent hour on Saturday so she could go out. It's her senior year in high school, and I want her to enjoy it, but I know music will always be foremost for her. In some ways she's an average kid; she's fun and silly and lively. These are great assets. Hopefully she won't change. Music is such a serious business, and opera is the worst; it's totally dog eat dog. It's a long haul to the top. There'll be many disappointments along the way.

Recently I saw a performance of hers and some other Julliard students at Carnegie Hall. The talent was unbelievable. I walked out of there in a daze. I loved it; I was so proud, but frankly, I feel I must hold her back. I want her to have a broader education, to attend a liberal arts college, to experience a normal campus life. She loves ceramics, she likes writing, so she needn't limit herself to music. I want more diversity in her life. She studies Italian and German, but of course that's for her opera training again.

She has to learn to stop herself, to pace herself, to calm herself, not to panic about time going by. There are days when she sings for an hour and a half straight and gets so keyed up and so exhausted she'll start crying. She must learn to stop pushing herself so hard. She has so much self-criticism and inner tension. I'm obsessive and perfectionistic myself, so I'm trying to learn to relax too, now that I see myself so clearly in her.

Through her I've acquired so much more understanding of music, especially of opera. I'm interested to see if she makes it; I want her to make it, but I don't want her to sacrifice her whole being in the process.

I was brought up in an Armenian home—a very strict home—and you went along with what your parents wanted. It was, "Yes Ma, no Ma. That's right, Ma." But kids do need a certain amount of discipline and direction. They had curfews and rules. I tried to make them fair, and it seemed to work most of the time. My son smoked pot in high school and drank a little beer but not to the point where it affected his studies or his personality so I went along with it. Karen, of course, doesn't because of her self imposed discipline, her voice.

I happen to like young people, the teen years are my favorite age. Their heads are good; they're much more interesting than many adults I know. So I enjoy most of their friends, but I did try to control their friendships on occasion. I would try to discourage them from seeing certain people. I would say, "Look at these people. What do you have in common with them?" There were times when they wanted to go places where I didn't know the parents, and I wouldn't allow them. My son would get angry, but I held fast, and he got over it in a couple of days. I was always aware of what they were doing because we're very family oriented. I do a lot with the kids. We never exclude them, even at our adult parties.

I'd ask them to help out around the house occasionally, and they would. They never got allowances; we just gave them what they needed. They did work outside the house. Tommy started working at fourteen as a dishwasher at our country club, Karen worked part time at fourteen too. It kept them busy and out of trouble. Tom now works summers as a tennis pro. I'm a tennis player, and I pushed tennis onto them a little. Football I hated, and I was glad when Tom gave it up, but I'm glad he found his own in tennis. Karen could have excelled in tennis too, but, of course, her music became more important, and I'm not disappointed.

My husband was pressured into going into the business because his parents started the store, and they worked very hard at it, but thank God, he's never pressured Tommy to go into it. It's a very lucrative business, but he would never put that stress on him. Tom has always had freedom of choice in his interests, and he has directed himself into the field he loves. My husband and I are of a different generation—we did what our parents wanted us to do—the Armenian ethics or whatever. Thomas has become interested lately in the Armenian culture. It seems that ethnic is "in," so many young people are interested in their roots now. Thomas spoke beautiful Armenian when he was young, but then I stopped speaking it so much around the house, and he lost his ability. Now I wish I had kept it up.

In keeping with my own Armenian upbringing I think I was a little overprotective. They depend a bit too much on me. They always ask me, "What do you think of this? What do you think of that?" Even though he's in college, Tommy always wants me to pick out his clothes. But it's also a compliment, a form of closeness. I'm now trying to give them more independence. Tommy's far away at college and may go to London next year on a Rhodes scholarship. I'd like to see Karen go to the midwest to school because she's too attached to her home. She's a delight to have around, and I'll miss her, but I think it would be better for her.

It's also time for me to get more involved in my own interests. The children have been the center of my life, but now I'm sort of excited about life without them. I've traveled with the children; we've been to Yugoslavia, to the Middle East, to the Caribbean, all over the states, but I'd like to travel more extensively. I want to expand myself in many ways.

I'm very strong willed, and I always wanted my youngsters to be the best. I stressed manners and still do. It's a very important part of life. I nagged them to do well in their studies, I made sure they only ate healthful foods. This all took a lot of nagging I'll admit, and it was hard to be consistent, hard to follow through, but eventually they assimilated most of my values.

I do admit when I'm wrong. I'm not afraid to change my mind if they convince me I've made a wrong or hasty decision. I also talk to them about my problems, my life, especially as they've gotten older. And I'll tell you something. They've got a good point of view, and I'm starting to listen to their advice, especially these last two years. I respect their intelligence and their openness. I was brought up to suppress my feelings, my thoughts, and I wanted them to be much more open than I was with my parents. So I tried to my utmost ability to answer their questions, yes, even about sex which was difficult for me.

Karen has not yet been sexually intimate with a boy, but

Tommy has a girlfriend who he sleeps with, and I'm not opposed to it. I approve of young people living together if they're not being coerced into it, if they really want to of their own volition, not just because it's the thing to do. I've seen a lot of young couples living together, and they have wonderful relationships. I think it makes much more sense than the way we were brought up. My God, to be married to someone you don't even know and expect it all to be rosy! My husband, of course, does not agree, especially for his daughter, and we argue about it. But I'm the one who brought them up, and he sees the end results, so he's beginning to agree more with my philosophies.

For example, my husband wants them to marry Armenians, and I don't care. For one thing, it's not practical to try to make them marry Armenians in this day and age. They just don't meet that many. I wouldn't want them to marry blacks just because there would be too much hassle in their lives. My son has a friend, the most delightful Chinese girl. They're just friends, but I wish it would become more. I would love it— she's such a marvelous human being. I do think that coming from a decent family is important. Basic upbringing should correspond, but finally, it's their decision, their life.

TED and ELAINE

"We really don't know what we did. Maybe a lot of it was just luck. It wasn't always wonderful, but at least there was plenty of communication."

Ted and Elaine are affable but determined people with solid middle class values. They are in no way provincial however, perhaps because Ted's job with an insurance company kept them constantly on the move. As Ted put it, "Every promotion meant a move," and Ted was promoted a lot.

Elaine and Ted believe in strict role delineation. "A woman's work is woman's work and a man's work is something different." They raised their three children carefully, watchfully, but respected their privacy, uniqueness and independence. The Wilson home had few rules, most of them merely common sense—"Come home at a reasonable hour"—though communication was not only stressed, but almost required. And there were limits. When Betsy, a high school senior, decided to move out and live with a girlfriend, Elaine laid down the law and meant it. The Wilson's never threatened their children, but they were not afraid to act on what they said. They talked to their kids and encouraged them to talk back. The family still communicates regularly by phone and at their annual family get-together.

TED: They learned through our moving around so much that they can make friends anywhere.

ELAINE: They're not afraid to approach anything. They have confidence. They can travel alone. They can meet people.

Nothing seems to bother them. They could go to dinner with the president, and they can be very humble with other people. Our moving around was partially responsible for this confidence, plus our training.

TED: We tried to make a point of spending time with each of them by themselves. If I were going on business someplace, I would ask one of the boys if he wanted to go along. We'd have lunch someplace. Or if I had to go to the office on Saturday, I'd ask Betsy along, and we'd have breakfast someplace.

ELAINE: I did the same thing. I always took Betsy along shopping with me; and we'd stop and have lunch in a nice restaurant—not just a hamburger. She learned to handle herself in public. We definitely stressed manners.

We had a lot of concerned compassion and a lot of respect for them. We respect their privacy, their opinions. They all did their own thing. But we did have rules and they had to show respect for the rest of the family. We made sure no one touched things that belonged to somebody else. If they wanted to use something of somebody's, they had to ask. They had their own things in their own rooms.

TED: The boys had rules such as for driving a car. #1 *You yourself* drive the car—not a friend—unless you're in a situation where you can't; like if you've had too much to drink. And come home at a reasonable hour—and you know what a reasonable hour is. And they didn't abuse it.

ELAINE: We did stay up waiting for them. They always called if they couldn't get home, even when they were in their twenties, to tell us where they were. And it was always open house here. Their friends were welcome to spend the night. We never pushed anybody out. They always brought friends home, and we always liked their friends. To this day some of their friends still communicate with us. Every evening we all sat around the dinner table; often the kids would invite their friends, and nobody wanted to leave. Everybody had their turn to talk. We always ate dinner together. We made a point of it.

I took care of everything during the dinner. I don't like everyone hopping up and down like yo-yos. The dinner hour was a peaceful, private time for the family. Because I didn't work outside of the house, I made sure Ted didn't have any work to do when he came home tired. I even mowed the lawn and weeded the gardens so we could have our weekends free to enjoy together. The boys were never expected to do dishes or ironing or anything like that. They didn't have to pick up their clothes or clean their rooms. They did work in the yard, and my daughter helped me with the housework.

TED: We believed that a woman's work is a woman's work, and a man's work is something different. They all held summer jobs, but not with our encouragement. I used to tell them, "You'll be a worker and a grown-up for a long time. Why don't you take the summer off?" But they wanted to work. They were hustlers, I guess.

ELAINE: Yes, we both always said, "You're a child for a very short period of time. Enjoy it. Go out and have some fun." Fortunately we always got them away in the summertime— we always went to Martha's Vineyard. And in the winter we would have winter picnics. We'd pack up the kids and some sandwiches and chicken legs and go to the beach.

We never involved them with our problems. We did not discuss how much Ted made or what we had. Whatever they wanted they had. They got allowances, nothing extravagent, and they had their chores, nothing heavy. We let them be independent. If they wanted help, it was available. But they were encouraged to do things on their own. The boys held jobs, brought home money, not to us, but for their own needs. They bought their own cars. Ted paid the insurance of course, because he worked for an insurance company, and he could get a discount.

TED: I used to joke a lot with all of them. The whole family joked a lot. That got us through hard times. They were allowed to make fun of me too, though they respected me so much it could get to be a burden. They relied on me, and they still do. It's flattering. They talked to us rather than go to anyone else.

I said to the kids, "You've got lots of pals. I'm not your pal or your buddy, I'm your father. You only have one father and you need one. Everyone needs a father." I had one, and I liked mine. And I think my kids liked me.

ELAINE: I arranged everything in our life around Daddy (Ted). The kids respected both of us. There was never any slurring around the house, but there was plenty of communication.

Our second son, Bill, went through a period where he wouldn't speak to anyone in the house for sometimes a week. We'd ask him, "What's troubling you? What's on your mind?" He'd say, "Well, I don't want to talk about it." We'd let this go on for a few days and finally I'd say, "Look, you're living in this house. Whatever your problem is, if you don't want to tell us, it's not our problem. If we're not the problem, then you can start acting like a human being because you're still living here. If we are, start communicating, talk to us, so we can do something about it."

TED: I used to be an athlete myself. I like sports. Bob, the first boy, was very good at sports. Bill, the second boy, was good enough; he wasn't bad. He made the football team in Maryland, but he came to me one day and said, "Hey, would you get very upset if I quit football?" I said, "No, why should I get upset?" He said, "Well, you know Bob is so good, and I know you like sports so much, I thought you might get upset if I quit." I said, "Heck, I don't care Bill." And he quit immediately. He was happy as a lark from then on. He just didn't want to play football anymore. I was a little surprised that he thought I would be upset that he quit. Sports should be fun. Too many parents push their kids. These men who get together and try to live out their fantasies . . . they're no longer athletes, they're too old for that. Sports becomes a gratification for the parents. It's not fun for the kids.

But you can't have children without having problems. Our main ongoing problems were with Betsy, our daughter, like smoking the marijuana and stuff.

ELAINE: Yes, she went through a period of lying because of this. She was supposed to be baby sitting, and we'd call her, and she wouldn't be there. Someone else would be baby sitting for her. She didn't dress properly; she didn't care how she looked. She started sleeping a great deal. I had trouble waking her up. She was fourteen when all this started.

TED: We had problems ourselves growing up. We understood. But I'll admit I got angry the first time I discovered it. I bumped into her in the park, and I knew immediately she was stoned, and oh boy, was I upset. She knew it, and she didn't like me to be angry, none of them did. But I didn't threaten her. I didn't say, "If you don't stop we're through with you." You can't bring yourself to that position if you're a parent. You don't want to get to a point where you say, "If you don't, we're going to do so and so," unless you mean it. But we did say we were disappointed in her. I spoke to her about our feelings about it. Then, fortunately we got transferred in her senior year in high school. She got away from the bunch of people she was hanging around with. I'm sure when she got to Michigan she still smoked, but it was different. She was older. She was definitely no longer abusing it.

ELAINE: But then, with three months to go till graduation, she came home from school one day and said, "I'm moving out. I'm going to get an apartment with my girlfriend Debbie." I said, "Fine. You've been giving us nothing but a bad time. I'll help you pack. But let me tell you one thing. You leave this house, you don't come back. You can spend the rest of your life with Debbie. Don't come back here for something to eat, or to borrow the car, or anything else. You walk out that door, and you're through. But you're going to wait until your father comes home to leave. I've given you eighteen years of my life, you can give me three hours of yours so sit here and wait for your father." When Ted came home he said to her, "Sit down!" And he gave her what for.

TED: I said, "How are you going to support yourself? You're still a minor, and I'm still responsible for you." She didn't go. It was a mood. Betsy's emotional. She's a redhead you know.

I sent all three of them to college, but I quit financing Betsy when she took field hockey as a subject and flunked. She was having a jolly good time. And I refused to finance her any more. So she came back and lived with us in Cleveland for a year and saved some money and went back to school on her own.

ELAINE: She came to Cleveland the first day and said, "Take me downtown to get a job." She went to the Higbee company in her blue jeans and got a job then and there. She started work the very next day. Nothing fazed her.

TED: Then she went back to college and moved in with her boyfriend, which we didn't care for even though we liked the boy very much. We went there one weekend and took her and her boyfriend out to lunch. Actually it was a champagne brunch. He brought it up when we'd had a few glasses of champagne and Betsy and Elaine went to the ladies room. He said, "Look, I know what we're doing is not right. I don't like it. I'm not that kind of a person." Apparently he wanted to get married, and she didn't. She wanted a career. So later, after more champagne, I said to both of them, "Make your mind up. Either get married or break up, or somebody will get badly hurt."

ELAINE: The next night they called to say that they were getting married, but Betsy said she didn't want a big wedding. So we sent them the money to use for other things.

I don't approve of living together before marriage. There's no honeymoon left after that. All three of our children are happily married—so far. They've had problems, but they try to work them out. They don't throw up their hands and quit any more than we did.

TED: Too many people are afraid to handle problems. You have to talk. You have to communicate. We still talk to the kids on the phone almost every week. And everyone comes home no matter where we are, for Christmas and the fourth of July. We have a major croquet tournament every fourth. It's called the Wilson Open or the Wilson Invitational. We have a cup. We award trophies. We have T shirts and various rules, like no drinking before 5 in the morning, etc.

ELAINE: Betsy has a good job working for the University of Michigan where she went to school. Her house is immaculate. The boys have good jobs, Bob works for his father's company, and both boys are helpful to their wives around the house. In fact, we think too much so.

TED: We really don't know what we did. Maybe a lot of it was just luck. It wasn't always wonderful, but at least there was plenty of communication.

THERESA

"But when I think of the things we did for the kids—we didn't do them for the kids. We did everything for ourselves, and they just managed to hang in there."

Theresa had her first child when she was nineteen. She's now an energetic, young grandmother of three, with another grandchild on the way. She teaches high school. Her husband Anthony is a painter and runs an art gallery.

Theresa and Anthony were both raised in an "Italian ghetto," both were always ambitious, creative, and adventurous. They married young and impetuously and set about enjoying their married life to the fullest. They spent all their free time with their children doing a myriad of interesting activities, leading a somewhat nomadic but cultural existence. Theresa says she "grew up" with her children. Still, Theresa and Anthony managed to maintain a subtle parent-friend separation and firm discipline. They reacted strongly and emotionally to the "slight problems" of "marijuana, petty burglary," etc.

Theresa attributes much of her success with her children to the example set by her own family, their closeness, their protectiveness, their warmth. Theresa's children all are married. Lisa is an elegant young matron, mother of two; Terry, an ebullient mother to be; Paul is a chef in a famous restaurant and a devoted father. Theresa is proud of them all and of their "healthy, productive lives." All of them still live in the neighborhood, sharing their adulthood with their mother and father, never losing that cherished sense of family that Theresa handed down to them.

Before I had kids I had no idea how I was going to raise them. I think I was too young. I was a child myself. I didn't realize it, but I was. I was only nineteen when I had Lisa. Lisa was twenty-seven when she had her first child. When I thought about Lisa growing up, I would have been horrified if she had had a child at nineteen. She was still such a baby. Raising children was a natural, instinctive thing. It was almost animalistic, it wasn't even thoughtful. I had no idea. I just did everything instinctively. There's no question: you nurse a baby, you change a baby, you take the baby to the doctor.

When they got to be teenagers, I played it by ear for the most part. I think what was very important is that Anthony and I never fought each other on anything. We were always together on things, we supported each other whether we agreed with each other or not. We argued a lot in private about what the kids were doing or weren't doing. But they never saw it. They always saw a united front. They never thought for a minute they could go to one or the other and get a different kind of treatment. That was instinctive also. We never really had any kinds of plans. . . . We never said, "This is the way we'll do this, or this is the way we ought to do that." It was sort of understood that we expected a certain behavior from them; and it was, after all, modeled a lot on what our parents expected from us. We had no other experience to model it after. It's different when parents nowadays go to business or have careers, take sociology courses in college, and child psychology courses, and have all prefixed notions. It wasn't that way with our generation.

I didn't work when my kids were little, not outside the home. I went back to work when the girls and Paul were seven, eight and nine years old. I was a shop-girl in a department store. I was out of the house but only while they were in school. Then I was home, or my mother was home, or Anthony was home. No, I was never out of the house that much, and then I worked right in the same neighborhood where we lived in Brooklyn so I walked to and from home, and I was

very close by. What I'm saying is we paid pretty close attention. One of us was always around. We spent a lot of time
with our kids, a lot of time—every Sunday, the city, to the
docks, to see the big boats, to museums, to parks.

We never said we ought to take our kids to museums because they ought to see beautiful paintings. We loved paintings so we took them. We loved to see the boats so we took the
kids. We never thought, "Let's take the kids to see the boats
because it will be good for the kids to see the boats." We
wanted to see them too. And in a sense we were kids ourselves. I was doing a lot of the things when I was raising the
children that I never got to do myself as a kid because we were
kind of ghetto-bound, and there was never the money or the
people to take us anywhere. I remember my father's bachelor
brother from New Jersey used to come, and we were delighted whenever he came because he would take us to Central
Park and then to Nedick's for a frankfurter in New York.
That was a big deal. *A big deal!* So that, when we were raising
our own children, anything we did with our children I think
was an acting out, on our own, parts of things I wasn't able to
do when I was a kid. So being that young I think we kind of
grew up with our kids. Which is why we feel very close to
them because we're almost "the same age." A tremendous
closeness because we grew up together, almost. A sharing of
immaturity was a great help; a kind of naivete and innocence.
We had a lot of fun with them.

At the same time—which is something I see in teaching
too—there was always that separation. We were always parents and children. We were never friends, really. How we
maintained that is a mystery to me. I don't think that anyone
can say, "This is the way you do it." I think that you believe
certain things and you believe them so strongly and you live
that way. You exude it. There's an understanding. It's the
same way in school. I have a great time with my students; we
laugh and joke, but I am Mrs. L. no matter what. There's
always that wall. They never get closer than that, but I have a

great relationship with them. I love them. We laugh, and we learn together. I think it was the same with my kids; it was a natural thing.

Some people will say, "How do you know what to do with kids in school?" I don't know, and yet I *do*. If I didn't know, I shouldn't be there. For instance, we have a showcase in school right now that I suppose is a sign of the times. The home economics department put in the showcase a baby, a little newborn baby doll, in a packing crate with straw, and there's a sign above it saying, "Too bad babies don't come with directions." And that's, I think, a sign of the times when so many young girls are having babies out of wedlock, without a man around to share a total relationship with the baby, to establish some kind of male-female/mother-father image. But, I think that, two people together who have made a baby are going to share in raising the baby in an instinctive way. Love is instinctive. Alone I think it's tough, it's difficult, it's hard; and I think that's when lots of problems arise. There's no doubt there's a lot of pressure raising children, and if you don't have each other to look for some kind of relief. . . . The way Lisa says to Carlo in the middle of the night, "The babies are up, please get up and take these kids off my hands for an hour. I've got to get a few winks." And Carlo comes to relieve her.

What about these young girls who are having children fifteen, sixteen or seventeen years old? They don't want abortions. They are living the free sex life. They are freewheeling, and so they are having children. And they are alone. Some of them come to school and leave the children with their mothers. That might be one way to work it out, but it's really not the same kind of relief. I don't think you can relate to your mother the way you would relate to a man who has shared the forming of that baby.

Anthony and I went through a particularly traumatic time personally when our kids were adolescents. And we didn't lose it then. I don't know how we didn't . . . but we didn't lose it. We were separated for a while, we divorced, we remarried. And our kids came through that beautifully. They never lost sight of the fact that we loved them very much. One of the things, of course, that brought us together again was consideration for the children. Which is not to say that we didn't love each other very much. But I'm sure that one of the things that brought us right back together again, stronger than ever, was the children. That sense of family that I missed so much. It was gnawing at my heart. That sense of being with the children and with Anthony, because we shared so much together. We had come through so much together that there was a terrible sense of loss, almost a sense of mourning. It's hard to leave a man with whom you've borne children.

What happened with us was a tremendous learning process. We came right back together as happy as ever—stronger. We had slight problems with each one of them at about the same age: marijuana, petty burglary. Suddenly the cops appear at your door. You straighten it out, and you go through it, and you think it's the end of the earth at the time. Looking back and understanding what young people are capable of getting into, you say, "Wow! we came through that, it was a horrible time!" And it's a good thing it appeared horrible because we reacted like crazy people. I went crazy and I would say, "What the hell is going on. . . ?" The emotional reaction I think is very important to kids too. To cool it and say, "Well now, let's sit down and talk about this," I think, kind of sanitizes the whole thing. And that's confusing to children who know they've done something wrong. With parents like us they expect an explosion, and they deserve it too. At the same time they understand that you're with them all the way, every minute. Very tricky. So that at the same moment you are venting your anger and satisfying yourself; at the same time your kid has to know that you're going to protect him from the outside world and help him through this. Don't tell me how you do it. I think you do it at the moment. It's like saying, "I don't know how I ever got through that. How the hell did I ever get through that?" It's like bearing the death of a loved one or coming through a particularly hard or painful time. Looking back you say, "I don't know how I ever did it." And it comes from some place inside.

But that some place inside has also been built up over the years. I had a fantastic mother and father, and we had a kind of family life that is almost out of Dickens: grey, poverty-stricken times and at the same time cheery during Christmas and holiday times. There were such opposites in our lives. I remember Saturday nights when there was only oatmeal for supper. At the same time when Christmas came, my father's bachelor brother came from New Jersey, and my mother managed to borrow a few dollars, here or there. There was a Christmas tree to the ceiling covered with stuff, presents for everybody. I remember other families in the neighborhood in the same situation as ours with lots of kids growing up in the depression, who had maybe coloring books for Christmas. Which is great if that's all you can do. We had bicycles and dolls, and we had only the best because my mother made sure that everything was always wonderful and fabulous.

Then when we were at the very bottom of things, there was still that kind of family relationship and love. We got preached to all the time: "Your brothers and sisters are your best friends. Don't go anywhere without a brother and sister. Don't leave your brother and sister behind. Don't let anybody talk about your brother and your sister. Don't let anybody hurt your brother and sister." So there was always this sense of family instilled in us. So wherever that strength comes from, inside, it was built up over the years, and I believe that for us—my brothers, and for me—it came from my parents.

And Anthony I think drew from his family a great sense of honor and loyalty and all this very rigid kind of stuff. So together, with my kind of free-wheeling, wild family and his kind, we complemented each other. At the same time, whenever there was a crisis, he always handled it. He would tell me, "Get off the phone, I'll handle this." And I understood why, and I did. I was too explosive. The kids would always say, "I can understand why Daddy had to take care of that." They are smart kids, too. I don't mean brilliant or intellectually smart, but I mean just a lot of common sense. I think that all the kinds of things that we suffered in our personal life strengthened us and the kids. It was very painful, but you learned from those things.

We're all human, and we all make terrible mistakes. The important thing I always said to the kids is learn from those mistakes. I look back on all the mistakes I made in my married life, and I hope never to make the same mistakes again, because of the pain that they caused. I only hope that everybody in the family—Anthony as well as the kids—all learn from the mistakes they have made. And I think that's really the most important thing. You have to learn from your mistakes. Don't do it again. That's all. Don't be stupid enough to do it again. If you know that it was bad and it was wrong and it was hurtful, don't be stupid enough to do it again.

I'm pleased with how my kids turned out. I don't think they could be better. I wish Paul were a little neater. I wish he were a better dresser; he's such a beautiful boy. But, I don't know, that's so minor. I think we have three of the greatest kids. We're always pleased to see them, love to have them around. They're entertaining. We're proud of them. They're not in any kind of trouble, thank God.

They're not like little robots. Lisa is very serious, very organized. Terry is really very happy, very funny but at the same time has that serious side; I know that she'll be fine with the new baby. I'm not worried about that at all. Paul is doing so nicely with himself, and he loves to cook, and he loves what he's doing; he seems to be such a solid kind of kid, and he's beautiful with his own kid.

There were always things, of course, that were bothering us about the kids. We always wondered how they would turn out. I was the first one in my family to have a college education. That's only because of my ego image of myself. I had to go and do it. I said, "I'm going to get a college education." I probably went for the wrong reasons. It turned out very well for me; but in no way did I ever expect my kids to attempt to do the same thing. Lisa went to college and finished. Terry went away for three months and came back. The same thing with Paul. That was perfectly allright. I don't think those two should have ever gone in the first place. I think Terry went just to get away from us at the time. She wanted to get out and go with her friends to Arizona where they were growing those wild mushrooms. They are different, and we in no way expected them to do what we ever did, or pattern themselves after us.

I always felt too—and I think this is very, very important—you have to raise your kids to leave you and lead their own lives, and they have a right to lead their own lives. As long as they are not hurting anyone, they are healthy, productive lives. So that when someone says, "Oh, you mean you didn't send him to college? What are you going to do about that?" I say, "Nothing. Let's see what the next move is."

We cherish our privacy, and we never minded their going, so they understood that. I don't know how or if we prepared them to be independent. We encouraged independence, but we had rules and regulations for them. Curfews. Not so much chores. They just naturally helped out. I liked to do things myself because no matter what they did I had to do it over again. I never liked the way they did it. I'd say, "Come on, let me do that, I'll finish that up. You go play." They were expected, however, to clean up their room and hang up their clothes. They couldn't be sloppy; they couldn't be piggy. If they did something in the kitchen, they cleaned up.

We never had any money so there was never a problem there; they never expected it from us. When they worked, they kept their own money, which was very different from our generation when we handed everything over onto the table because we were so destitute. By the time our kids were growing up, we were just beginning to save, believe it or not. Even though Anthony earned some money over the first fifteen years of our married life, it was just enough to subsist on because he was either always going to art school or we were trying to do different things with our lives.

For instance, we lived in the mountains one summer on twenty-five dollars a week. It was great for the kids but we didn't do it for them. We did everything for ourselves and they just managed to hang in there with us. We managed to come out here in the winters because we liked to be on the beach so much so we decided one summer, twenty-three years ago, to drive all the way out to the beach and just sleep on the beach for the weekend. Who was going to bother us? We never knew anything about police laws. We had a tent and we brought food, orange juice, bathing suits, underwear, everything. And we camped on the beach from Friday night until Sunday night. Lisa said to me just a few weeks ago, "Mommy, I can never forget those times; they were so wonderful." I said, "I'm glad because we had a great time too." But *we* were the ones who wanted to go to the beach. We didn't say to ourselves, "Let's do it for the kids." We did it really for all of us. We were the ones who wanted to go to the mountains. We were the ones who wanted to go to museums on Sunday. We really wanted to go too, we didn't do it out of sacrifice for the kids.

JEAN and ERNEST

"You don't make unreasonable rules; rules they can't follow or understand, or rules just to hurt them."

Jean and Ernest, both from large families themselves, always wanted a big and close knit family. They treated their children as responsible adults from the beginning. They were strict, but understanding, and never inspired fear or awe. Both of them credit the nature of farm life as conducive to togetherness and maturity, as well as being a lot of fun.

Jean, who worked as a nurse before her marriage, stayed home to raise her children, only returning when Patrick, her youngest, was ten. Jean and Ernest are devoutly religious. Their children all attended strict Catholic schools. Even though the three oldest children are now at college, they still attend church regularly.

As I was conducting this interview we were joined by Patrick, now thirteen, and his Irish Setter puppy. Patrick is energetic, bright, outgoing, totally unselfconscious and poised, and possesses a formidable vocabulary. Ernest and Jean showed no reticence in front of him and welcomed his contributions. As they spoke, he teased them, contradicted them, agreed with them, in short, proved himself a delightful example of the spirit and intelligence Jean and Ernest had hoped to instill.

ERNEST: We knew what they were doing twenty-four hours a day. We took vacations with them. We were always together. But we made them independent too.

JEAN: We treated them like human beings. We didn't talk to

them like children. As a matter of fact, we might have involved them in too much. I remember once Donny, our oldest, refusing to go to school because he wanted to help with the planting. He was so involved with our life, our finances, that he worried a lot.

ERNEST: We gave them responsibilities. Don liked tractors and stuff—he liked to drive. I gave him the responsibility of driving very early. This gave him confidence. It built his ego up. He preferred that to having a bicycle or a go-cart.

JEAN: Donny had dyslexia and couldn't read till about the 5th or 6th grade. Not too many people knew about dyslexia at that time. So his ego had to be maintained. When he was ten years old Ernie took him out to the barn and said, "O.K. Donny, here's an old tractor." And they took it apart and put it back together again. From that day on, Donny was tremendous with his hands. And that built his ego. I should say Ernie built his ego, like you wouldn't believe. He'd go into school and boast about driving a big tractor. He felt like he could do something the other kids couldn't.

ERNEST: He worked with us. We didn't overwork him, and he enjoyed it. Plus he got to know about responsibility, and it built his spirits.

JEAN: Every one of our kids were given a whole big patch, almost an acre, to grow vegetables on. Every night after school they'd all work and put the vegetables in. They'd hoe it and take care of it and harvest it, and then they'd put the vegetables on a little table out front to sell. The money was pooled for our trips together. The boys also went into a lawn mowing business.

Nancy didn't do as much on the farm, but she took riding lessons. We boarded a training horse here for a neighbor up the road, and she had that responsibility. She'd get up before school and muck out the stalls and then exercise it after school.

ERNEST: We tried to cultivate what they liked best. Like

Nancy liked horses, our boys liked sports. Greg and Donny both played football at St. Boniface High School. They both made the all-star teams—got a lot of awards and trophies. Patrick plays a good game of golf.

JEAN: They were also all into sailing. We bought them sunfishes. One was second hand, the other one they got from some old guy for a half a case of gin. We didn't give them lots of things until they went to college, and then we gave them each a truck—but of course that was for use on the farm too.

ERNEST: When they got to high school they had beer parties, but we had rules, curfews.

JEAN: And they had to obey those rules. One night when Nancy was about seventeen, she went to a party with Donny. He was a football player; she was a cheerleader. He was driving and keeping an eye on her. They always came in to say goodnight to us. Ernie used to make believe he was asleep. This night she was saying, "Oh, I had such a good time!" and I could tell she'd had too much to drink. So I said, "Shh, you'll wake your father up." So they went into the bedroom, and I heard her say, "Donny, the room's going around!" And he said, "Put your feet on the floor and shut up, you'll wake the old man." With that she fell out of bed. They thought it was a big joke.

The next day, Ernie got up early with Greg and went to a football game and came back around two o'clock in the afternoon. Nancy was dancing around to the stereo with her friends, having a good old time, and he walked up to her and said, "You're grounded for three weeks." Just like that. And she said, "WHY?" And he said, "Because you don't know how to put your feet on the ground." Of course, he had heard the whole thing. And he went in, and he sat down to read. She went in on her knees begging because she had tickets for a rock concert, but he wouldn't relent.

ERNEST: They got punished, they weren't angels. None of them smoked cigarettes, they've probably tried marijuana, but as far as drugs were concerned I assumed they were pretty free of them. I could tell if the boys had had too many beers. I'd tell them if they did that again, they couldn't use the pickup or the cars.

JEAN: We really stuck to our guns, but it was tough. Like it was the junior prom, and Donny was not old enough to drive at night. Lots of the parents were letting underage kids drive anyway because the prom was forty miles away. But we absolutely refused. We solved it by letting him drive himself and his date there while it was still light. Then we drove over later and parked next to his car and waited for them in the dark till the dance was through. They came out and slipped into the car just as if he was driving, and we drove them home. None of the kids ever knew. We still laugh about it. We always made sure to stick together on things.

ERNEST: You don't make unreasonable rules, rules they can't follow or understand, or rules just to hurt them. But when you have to be strict, you are. We never made rules about their friends or dates—they chose their own friends. Of course, they didn't have too many friends we didn't like. Usually their friends were excellent.

JEAN: But they did have friends who drove crazy. Greg had one friend—they left one night in his truck and about five minutes later they were back, and I saw them hop into Greg's truck and take off. Later I asked, "What happened?" And Greg said, "That guy will kill himself. I'll never drive with him again!" And I said, "Good! Don't ever do it."

But we let them all go their own ways. Nancy is the independent one. She used to talk about going to Hawaii and living on the beach. She was the first one to take her mattress off the frame and put it on the floor. It almost killed me, but I let her do it. I just closed the bedroom door.

We used to fight about the dishes and stuff, Nancy and I, but now we are so close. After she was away at college for a couple of months—she's at Smith—she wrote me a nice letter saying she realized how intelligent and wonderful I am. She calls twice a week. She's such a cute kid. We're friends now. For awhile we were just mother and daughter, but she grew up and now we're friends. She called last night and told me Doris, her roommate, and she were going to get an apartment in Chicago when they graduate. And I said, "That's wonderful. I'll have a place to stay when I want to go see the shows." She said, "Doris' mother is in a state of shock and is refusing to talk to her. She's so hurt and angry that Doris is moving away from her." But I know that Nancy and I couldn't live together. She's got to be her own person.

ERNEST: They have to make their own way after they get their education. They have to lead their own lives. Donny wants to get a job in engineering and live with us a year or two until he has his feet on the ground. That's fine. He can do some work around here to pay his way. In fact, I'll even pay him if he'd like to work extra.

JEAN: My boys and Ernie, too, have said that they can do a lot of thinking and praying while they're out there on that tractor. Greg, especially, says he works out a lot of problems that way. They enjoy farming so much that both boys say they would love to be farmers, but the money hassles are too much. Donny plans to work in engineering till he's about fifty, become a millionaire, retire, and have a farm for a hobby. They're planners all of them, they plan for the future; they look ahead.

We didn't get married until our mid-thirties, and it was very hard for me to adjust to living away from my mother. It was so hard for me to break away that I make sure to encourage them to look to the future even if it means moving away from here. We have to face that fact that there are very few opportunities in this area. So we'll give them the very best in college educations, and then we'll have to let them go. I don't want their breaking away to be as painful as mine was.

We are Catholics, but we wouldn't care if they married non-Catholics. It would only bother us, especially Ernie, if they married a black. As a matter of fact, Nancy's been going with a Jewish boy, and he treats her nice. I would like to see them stay in the faith themselves in some form.

ERNEST: You can't pick their husbands and wives for them. It's their choice. They have to live with that person. There is no way you can influence them once they're in school, they're on their own. It's their life now, and whatever they want to do with it, it's up to them.

JEAN: My mother, she was an old Polish lady, had an expression, "You burn your ass, you sit on the blister." Like Greg called the other night from Cornell and said, "I'm having a lot of trouble with physics, and I want to drop it." I said, "What do you mean?" He said, "I've talked to my advisor, and he says I'm in the wrong class. Should I drop it or get a tutor?" I said, "It's your decision. Whatever you decide is allright with me. But I'm not going to tell you whether to drop it or not." I encourage them to think for themselves. Donny started out wanting to be a mechanic, and we didn't say no, but he decided to try one semester in college, and now he's enrolled in a five year engineering course.

I didn't go back to work until Patrick was ten. Then I only worked part time. The kids never even knew I was a nurse or that I had a master's degree. They did notice that I knew how to make a bed!

When I started working, Ernie would have my martini and dinner waiting for me when I got home. He took a lot of enjoyment from my work, and the kids loved to listen to stories about the patients. We all participate in each other's lives. Donny works at the beach in the summer as a lifeguard, and he's very good looking, and fourteen and fifteen year old girls call him all the time. I was concerned that he was going out with such young girls. But Greg said, "Mom, Donny's sexual maturity is late. He's just realized he's got a body. Give him time."

The kids are very close. The first three are only thirteen

months apart. The two of us wanted to go to Ireland this June, and we told them about it. They called us immediately and said they had it all arranged. They would run the farm and take care of Patrick while we were gone. Patrick talks to his brothers and sister all the time. He calls Donny in Florida for some advice about girls. I'd love to know what the advice is. When they all went off to school, Patrick felt very depressed. He thinks it's boring without them here. He has a great time when they're home for the summer—swimming, sailing, hanging around with them and all their friends. They take walks, they play backgammon. When they all leave, Patrick says, "I feel homesick without leaving home."

Our family is closer now than they've ever been. Nancy especially feels that way. She had more fun with the family this summer than ever before. They've always had to rely on each other for companionship because this area's so isolated.

Nancy has been a bit of a problem because she loves to spend money, she gets carried away—she wants this, she wants that, and all very expensive stuff. We try to insist that she earn money for her personal use. She won a $5,000 scholarship to Smith—she's always been such a bright girl, but still it's expensive.

Donny never asks for money—in fact he gives most of the money he earns to us. And he has jobs at college to earn extra money. During the summer Greg works as a lifeguard during the day and is a bartender at night. Patrick has a job taking care of our neighbor's dogs. He puts the vegetables he grows out on the stand, and he cuts lawns. He's already saving money for his college tuition. We never gave the kids allowances, but we gave them responsibilities that earned cash.

ERNEST: If they ever needed money or had any other problems, they were always free to come and talk to us. I told them, talk to us first. And they were not afraid to discuss anything with us. And we never acted shocked by anything they told us.

I also told them not to be afraid to ask questions. That's the only way you are going to learn. How are you going to learn if you don't ask?

JEAN: And if they asked us something we didn't know, we'd all look it up together. As you see, we have three complete sets of encyclopedias—for every age level.

I know this all sounds like a story book, but it's all true. We had our fights, we had our discussions, but mostly it was wonderful. We had so much fun. I loved it. It's been great.

CONCLUSION

Is there a formula for successfully raising teenagers? Are there any specific answers? Yes, and no. Parents vary, children vary, circumstances vary. But basic parental expectations seem similar—good grades, good health, freedom from drug and alcohol abuse, help with household chores, consideration for others. And of course, love and respect toward the parents. Fortunately, there are some ways to achieve this. Unfortunately, the ways involve endless patience, consistency, reappraisal, and a lot of hard and sometimes tedious work.

The most outstanding answer involves structure: rules, curfews, familial responsibilities. Most parents emphasized manners, those who didn't wished they had. Most except the very wealthy demanded help with household chores and part time jobs outside the house to help defray expenses for college or personal necessities and luxuries. The nature of the rules varied: behavior that was acceptable to Jessica or Justine was definitely not acceptable to Jean and Ernest or Francesca. Whatever rules were made, though, were made to be followed. Moira's rules forbid impertinence; Anne Marie's, drugs and drinking; Anita's, foul language. But each effective parent did know what was important to them, how to stick to their guns, how to instill certain values. Rules should be minimal, should involve simple consideration for other people, or designed to prevent physical or mental danger. But they must exist.

ERNEST: "When you have to be strict you are."

JACK: "The biggest mistake we made with (our daughter) is that we were not strict enough. We let her tyrannize us."

BILL: "If I felt it was a life threatening situation, I would forbid it."

JESSICA: ". . . although my rules were kept to an absolute minimum, mostly rules of consideration—calling when you're going to be late, helping out around the house—they were enforced."

BARBARA: "It took a lot of nagging I'll admit, and it was hard to be consistent, hard to follow through, but eventually they assimilated most of my values."

CLAUDIA: "I was not well cast for the role (of disciplinarian), but I did it."

JIM: "I think there's a way of just lovingly having expectations of what someone has to do and making them do it; . . . not being nasty but strict."

The majority of teenagers need close supervision, homework monitored, friendships sometimes censored, drugs, cigarettes, alcohol, if not forbidden, strictly controlled. Many parents praised athletics as a healthy outlet, both as a way of "keeping them busy" and as an asset to physical well being. While some parents admitted to "discouraging" certain friends, not one said they would ever interfere with the choice of a romantic partner.

ANITA: "When my son . . . went to live with his girlfriend, I couldn't be critical of that. I had to respect his decision. I knew he wouldn't live with just anybody."

ERNEST: "You can't pick their husbands and wives for them. It's their choice. They have to live with that person. There is no way you can influence them."

FRANCESCA: ". . . the one thing I would never interfere with was their romances. I let them go out with whoever they liked. . . . You can't hold your kids back in these things; otherwise you'll lose their love."

The question of formalized religion is a toss-up. Some families emphasized it, many did not. But those who did made sure to follow through and set an example.

HELEN: "My kids all went to church. I insisted on that. And not only that, but I insisted that my husband and I set an example. I didn't believe in sending them off to Sunday School and us reading the paper or staying in bed later. We went too, every Sunday."

CONSTANCE: "My girls were exposed to a non-denominational religious organization that I and my brother had been involved in over the years. . . . The girls were inspired, influenced; and after that we began to share."

ANNE MARIE: "We have very strong faith. I tell them if there's nothing else in life, we have a very strong belief in God."

Setting an example comes up again and again. Teenagers learn essential lessons from their parents.

BILL: "They learned good behavior by example, not by force."

HANK: "(my daughter) . . . has an inner gyroscope that will carry her through. I think I gave her that."

JOANNE: "I tried to set a good example for (my son). I taught him how to save money, to make money. . . . I taught him good manners and how to treat a woman."

JACK: "I believe in what you can create yourself. That's more important than all the abstractions of fame and success and riches. That idea was gotten home pretty thoroughly."

JOHN: "Some of his sensitivities (my son) . . . picked up from me. I've contributed my sense of irony, a sense of humor, a certain awareness of inequality and unfairness."

JESSICA: ". . . the good thing (my son) learned from me—and his father—is to be truly a tolerant and humanistic person. . . . I think he gained his social graces, his tact, his diplomacy, his sincere interest in others, from us. . . ."

CONSTANCE: "I think my forte was my confidence about, and love for, parenting. I believe this is the strongest point I have passed on to my four children. No matter how many issues to be worked out or questions of life to be answered . . . parenting is most important."

Family closeness—togetherness—is important. Even the busiest parents mentioned having a compulsory evening meal together.

ANITA: "We did a lot of things together at home. We ate dinner together every night—that was a must."

THERESA: "We spent a lot of time with our kids. . . . Every Sunday—to the city, to the docks, to see the big boats, to museums, to parks."

MICHAEL: "There was a good amount of family life. We would go to the city together, we'd travel. We'd visit relatives."

ELAINE: "Every evening we all sat around the dinner table; often the kids would invite their friends. . . . Everybody had their turn to talk. We always ate dinner together. We made a point of it."

ESTHER: "We insisted of familial responsibilities, like attending family functions. We came together at the dinner table. We ate together and talked about the day."

JOHN: "I spent a lot of time with (my son). We watched T.V. together. We discussed events, common experiences. We talked about my work; I've always tried to interest him in what I'm doing."

HELEN: "(We) did a lot of things with the kids. We went to all their sports events. We took an interest in everything they did. We always planned family vacations."

ERNEST: "We knew what (the kids) were doing twenty-four hours a day. We took vacations with them. We were always together."

JOANNE: "My son and I always did things together. I took him to Broadway shows, we learned how to ski. . . . We took karate together. . . . We saved our money . . . and went to Mexico for two weeks."

EILEEN: "I would dream up excursions and things to do. . . . We'd go to the beach, we'd go to the movies . . .we'd play games."

Siblings, extended family, or a close network of good friends can help make a parent's job much easier.

HELEN: "We had . . . two grandmothers living here during their teenage years, and they were marvelous. They were never too tired to pay attention to the children, they were always very tolerant of them, very loving to them. The kids loved having them here . . . they learned a lot from each other. And it was really a help to me"

JESSICA: "(My son) and I often lived with other people. There were other people, specifically my brother, and other women around for him to talk to. And this saved the day."

ELIZABETH: "For whatever reason, (my daughter) needed adult substitutes—people to talk to."

SYLVIA: "(My daughter) also has adult friends that she relates to well, a number of women friends of mine that she visits. She seeks them out when she has problems."

RACHEL: "Since Jane is my closest friend, I felt tremendously relieved that (my daughter) had someone to talk to because I knew she really needed it."

Therapy and therapists were also helpful to both teenagers and parents when problems arose. Parents speak of the "helping professions" with gratitude and respect.

CONSTANCE: "My son found a fantastic therapist . . . who gathers people around and imparts knowledge of a certain way of life. This group therapy has really helped him . . . to relate better to other people."

MOLLY: "The intensity of (my son's) rebellion was so painful to me, I often wanted out, but his psychologist kept reminding me of how important it was to follow through, to keep showing (him) I cared. Great advice, because I was not at all in touch with this."

MEG: ". . . I needed help. I went to a women's group and they pointed out I was trying to be a madonna. They would say, 'Doesn't that bother you when your kids act like that?' And all of a sudden I'd realize, 'Yes, maybe that does bother me'."

BILL: "I was very lucky that I was able to stop drinking . . . with the help of a lot of people I was able to do it. I learned a whole value system from A.A. (Alcoholics Anonymous), and my life is much better."

BRUCE: "Then I started to straighten out. . . . I had to get honest. I had to tear everything off to see what I was made of. I was in intense therapy, and I was in A.A."

The message is clear; don't be afraid to seek help from outside sources.

Parents unanimously stressed honesty, communication and a willingness to learn from their children.

FLORENCE: "Both my daughters were pretty verbal and spoke up. . . . From watching and listening I had a pretty good idea of what was important to them."

PETER: "I never avoided (my stepson's) problems. I never avoided talking to him."

TED: "Too many people are afraid to handle problems. You have to talk. You have to communicate."

JUSTINE: "(My son) asked me once before he went to high

school what a guidance counselor was. So I was telling him, and he said, 'Oh you mean they provide you with counselors in school like I've always had personally with you?'"

JOHN: "I always talked to (my son), engaged him in conversation, was always myself in front of him."

CLAUDIA: "(My stepson) and I would have dinner out together, I would be sure to ask him about his life, girls at school, and all of that."

ANITA: "I was honest with the children in every sense, like even them knowing what we could afford. . . . They knew our circumstances at all times. I never hid anything—if something had to be said, I said it."

ERNEST: If (the kids) have ever needed money or had any other problems, they were always free to come and talk to us. . . . And they were not afraid to discuss anything. . . . And we never acted shocked by anything they told us."

JUDY: "(My daughter) now tells me a whole lot. We talk about our sex lives pretty openly. I try to do that because I want to make sure she's getting everything she can."

RACHEL: "(My daughter) and I started talking about one in the afternoon . . . and we sat there talking till nightime. She asked me all the questions she had on her mind."

HANK: "There are horrible things happening to me. I'm quite lonely, and things go wrong in my life. . . . So while I don't use (my daughter) as a sympathizer I try to tell her how things are with me."

MEG: "On each of the kids' sixteenth birthday I sat down and had a long talk with them. We don't have any rites of passage in this culture. So on their sixteenth birthday I would get them a really major gift, and we'd also have a major talk."

ELLEN: "We listened to (the kids) words. Very important—you must *listen*—not half-heartedly overhear what they're saying."

BARBARA: "I talk to (the kids) about my problems, my life. . . .

And I'll tell you something. They've got a good point of view, and I'm starting to listen to their advice."

But Bruce says it best, most definitively, of all.

"So the honest communication is very important—to be really risk taking, to be willing to say, 'Sometimes I don't feel good about myself. I'm very often afraid. I have the same fears you have. I want you to turn out perfect because I'm so far from perfect.' Admit to your own imperfections. The teenager wants desperately to be respected. Don't look down. Meet your teenager eye to eye the way I finally met my son."

These mistakes, these imperfections, are human, inevitable, and not irreparable.

MEG: "I made definite mistakes, but I didn't stop at that. I had to go on even when I expected the worst. And I grew up with my kids. As I learned about myself, moved forward myself, I was able to help them do the same."

BRUCE: "There are still remnants of the past . . . memories of my mistreatment. . . . But (my son) sees a father who wants to get better—who wants to get closer with him, who wants to be more real. And he's able to say, 'Let's pay attention to what's happening now. . . . I don't forget those things, but look at the relationship we're capable of having today. Let's go for the best we can.'"

Many parents said they were friends with their children. All of them spoke of mutual respect and the necessity of maintaining the "tricky" separation between friendship and parental authority.

RACHEL: "We did not want to be close friends—we wanted to be mother and daughter. My life was mine, and hers was hers."

MOIRA: "I remember saying (to my daughter), 'If I have to

sacrifice a friendship in order to be the authority right now, I'll do that.'"

THERESA: We had a lot of fun with (the kids). At the same time—there was always that separation. We were always parents and children."

MEG: "The children needed something definite from me, not for me to be just one of the boys."

TED: "I said to the kids, 'You've got lots of pals. I'm not your pal or your buddy, I'm your father.'"

JIM: "The difficulties I had with my boys minding me also came from my trying to be a buddy to my kids rather than a father."

And when problems arise, as they certainly will with teenagers, effective parents recommend direct action. Different solutions, of course, for different people in different circumstances.

MOLLY: "If you have a problem to figure out just start doing something. Keep weeding out the wrong answers till you see what the right ones are."

HELEN: "One time (my son) was rude to me, he was fresh, he snapped at me and his father slapped him right in the face."

SYLVIA: "(My daughter) did sneak out of the house once with a young man. . . . She was grounded for an entire month."

FRANCESCA: "And I said (to my son), 'John, I can spot it, I can smell it, and if you walk into this house on pot, I'll take you to a reformatory, and I'll throw you in.' And I meant it. I would have."

JESSICA: "The few times (my son) did disobey me, I went after him. Literally. I dragged him out of a movie I had forbidden him to see by his hair; I called the police one night when he didn't call in, and I would order him home from friend's houses if he hadn't cleaned his room properly."

JACK: "When (my daughter) came in here weeping with five F's on her God damn report card and not even a single note from the teachers saying, 'Please see me or anything' . . . we moved the whole family immediately . . . to England."

THERESA: "To cool it and say, 'Well now, let's sit down and talk about this,' I think, kind of sanitizes the whole thing. And that's confusing to children who know they've done something wrong. With parents like us they expect an explosion, and they deserve it, too."

JIM: "I would say to say to someone who is having difficulties. . . , don't wait until it's too late. If things are getting too hot and too hectic, think of some solutions that would involve a different environment, a better environment, an environment in which someone can learn."

Expectations are o.k.; they're inevitable, perhaps desirable.

MICHAEL: "My expectations were general, but the children knew I wanted them to have some direction in life."

ALAN: "(Our children) saw different standards and interests and commitments to social issues which were important to us. There was a . . . withholding of respect for the values we didn't have."

SYLVIA: "I would like her to finish four years of college because I did not. I'd like her to finish and have a degree, and I think she will."

ELIZABETH: "I have strong ideas of who I am and what I want, and that's helpful for kids because there's not ambivalence."

ED: "We were demanding about (the boys) performance in school—god damned demanding—and they did well because of this. They did well because it was expected of them."

JUSTINE: ". . . mostly I'm interested in him being as psychologically healthy as possible. That's my main expectation of him. I won't be particularly disappointed if he doesn't achieve a certain kind of success or a certain kind of marriage, or certain kinds of friendship patterns. I don't have an invest-ment in that. I just want him to be pleased with what he does. I don't want him to be neurotic and fucked up."

But parental expectations, though useful to adolescents as guidelines, must be subject to change and allow for eventual autonomy.

JOHN: "The trick to child raising is to try to relate to the child in such a way that you're influencing him or her to be as independent and as capable of becoming the person that he or she could become."

THERESA: "I always felt too—and I think this is very, very important—you have to raise your kids to leave you and lead their own lives."

MEG: "I was in this world to help them grow up to be mature people, not to keep them babies."

FLORENCE: "I always felt that as a parent one of my primary duties was to bring up children who could be independent people."

MICHAEL: ". . . I will say that I didn't expect my children to follow in my footsteps. They could do their own thing."

JEAN: "It was so hard for me to break away (from my mother) that I make sure to encourage them to look to the future even if it means moving away from here. . . . We'll give them the very best in college educations, and then we'll have to let them go. I don't want their breaking away to be as painful as mine was."

ELIZABETH: "I was very independent as a child, and I wanted my kids to do everything for themselves they could possibly do."

HANK: "(My daughter) has said to me, 'What do you want me to be? What do you want me to do?' I say, 'Nothing. I just want you to grow up and be happy, and you can pick out what you want to do'."

NORA: "You've done things, you've given (your children) things up to a certain point. They ought to be able to make it from there."

JUSTINE: "As (my son) slowly comes into himself, he'll have to make decisions on how he wants to live. We've given him a value structure as best we can, and it's up to him to take it."

ANITA: "You can't own (your children). You can love them and care for them, but you can't own them."

For most of these parents children were the main focus, the "center" of their lives. Most mothers did not work outside the home unless absolutely necessary. Even then, close family members usually took over; grandparents, siblings, or husbands. Constant attention, involvement and discipline were eseential elements in the child raising process.

It all sounds like very time consuming, very serious business. And it is. But perhaps the most important "rule" of all is to relax and enjoy it, to have a certain "immaturity" regardless of age, that allows you to have a good time with your teenager.

MEG: "My kids and I learned the hard way, but now I enjoy them immensely. I have fun with them."

JONAS: "(My stepdaughter) and I went from total hate, to her treating me cordially, and then to her actually liking and accepting me. I enjoy her now."

FLORENCE: "I thought they were interesting kids. I was interested in them, and our house was open to their friends, and I enjoyed meeting them."

BARBARA: "I happen to like young people, the teen years are my favorite age. Their heads are good; they're much more interesting than many of the adults I know."

RACHEL: "When (my daughter) came to visit on vacations, we laughed a lot, and we had fun. I actually looked forward to it."

TED: "I used to joke a lot with all of (the kids). The whole family joked a lot. That got us through hard times."

PETER: "(My stepson) would start describing some classical homosexual encounter, and I'd proceed to describe some equally ridiculous heterosexual encounter, And we'd both laugh. We'd get to it on a laughing level. I think that was very important—a sense of humor."

MOIRA: "My kids are gorgeous, They're heaven, They're fun."

CLAUDIA: "I took (my stepson) to buy his first suit. He was so excited, and I had a great time. The sales people were confused about our relationship which we enjoyed immensely."

JOANNE: "(My son) was so much fun to be with. I enjoyed every year, including the teenage years."

EILEEN: "The best time I ever had was (my son's) sixteenth birthday. I made a surprise party for him. I had his friends in cahoots with me."

THERESA: "(My daughter) said to me just a few weeks ago, 'Mommy, I can never forget those times; they were so wonderful.' I said, 'I'm glad because we had a great time too.'"

JEAN: "We had our fights, we had our discussions, but mostly it was wonderful. We had so much fun. I loved it. It's been great."

Thanks. . . .

To Martin and Judy, for their inspiration, their advice, their patience.

To Charisma, for typing and more.

And especially to Bruce, who endured.

For a free catalogue of other titles write
THE PERMANENT PRESS
RD 2 Noyac Road
Sag Harbor, N.Y. 11963